A
WOMAN'S DIARY
OF THE WAR
SARAH B. MACNAUGHTAN

1915

Contents

PREFACE

"I am rather surprised to find how little the quite young girls seem to mind the sight of wounds and suffering. They are bright and witty about amputations, and do not shudder at anything. I am feeling rather out-of-date amongst them."

So wrote Sarah Broom Macnaughtan of her service in war as a nurse.

The horror of World War I was unleashed on July 28, 1914 and lasted until November 11, 1918. More than 9 million combatants and 7 million civilians died. It was a global conflict of horrendous conditions exacerbated by technological advancements in armaments and stalemated trench warfare. Macnaughtan was an early participant.

Sarah Macnaughtan was born on October 26, 1864 in Partick, Scotland (today a part of Glasgow), the fourth daughter and sixth child of Peter Macnaughtan and Julia Blackman, she was home schooled by her father. Her parents died and she moved to Kent in England, then to London. There she began to write, with her first novel, *Selah Harrison*, being published in 1898. Her best-known works were *The Fortune of Christina M'Nab* (1901), *A Lame Dog's Diary* (1905), and *The Expensive Miss Du Cane* (1900). She traveled to Canada, South America, South Africa, the Middle East and India. Sarah participated in the women's suffrage movement, aided victims of the Balkan war, performed social services for the poor in London's East End, and worked for the Red Cross during the Second Boer War.

During the outbreak of the First World War, she volunteered with the Red Cross Society. In September 1914 she travelled to Antwerp in Belgium as part of an ambulance unit. For her work under fire in Belgium, she received the Order of Leopold. Later in the war she began a journey to Russia where she planned to provide medical assistance. However, during the trip through Persia she became ill and had to return to England, where she died on July 24, 1916. She was buried in the family plot in Chart Sutton, a small village on the edge of the Weald of Kent, southeast England.

An unfinished manuscript became the basis for her book, *My Canadian Memories*, which was finished by her friend Beatrice Home and published in 1920. MacNaughtan Road in Leaside (near London) was named after her.

CHAPTER I.

LONDON.

HARDLY anyone believed in the possibility of war until they came back from their August Bank Holiday visits and found soldiers and sailors saying good-bye to their families at the stations. And even then there was an air of unreality about everything, which rendered realization difficult. We saw women waving handkerchiefs to the men who went away, and holding up their babies to railway carriage windows to be kissed, and we saw pictures of this afterwards in next morning's journals; but that the thing which we had talked about, and laughed at, and sung funny songs about, was really going to happen, and that we were going to war with Germany, seemed incredible for a time. We were breathless, not with fear, but with astonishment.

Most of us will remember that a summer of very fine weather had just passed. The long light days and the sunshine are already inseparably connected in the minds of some of us with the thought of last times, which makes the memory of the summer exceptionally dear to us. Already the blooming of roses suggests days that will not come again, and the memory of lives that were more to us than a thousand Junes.

On a certain radiant morning before the hay was mown, we learned that a man and woman had been murdered in a distant country. Murder has a particularly horrible sound about it on a summer morning with red roses in bloom. We felt deeply for a great family who had known many tragedies, and we said sorrowfully that here was another awful happening to an ill-fated house. For a woman done to a violent death also we felt pity and horror. But the murder was an historic event and not a personal one, and after a time it was forgotten or left undiscussed. Events did not happen quickly after the deaths of the Grand Duke and Duchess of Austria. To royal houses such things, with all their tragedy, had happened before and might happen again. There was nothing to show that the world was astir with amazing possibilities, and there was no whisper sent forward of the news that was to follow. Sometimes it seems

3

possible that our own statesmen knew less of the things that were to happen in the immediate future than did even the common man who is called the " man in the street." The man in the street had often scented war, and war-scares at this time were regarded as the special prerogative of harmless lunatics. Books and pamphlets on Germany and the German invasion had ceased to be interesting, in view of the fact that across the narrow strip of water that divides England from her Celtic sister there was more than a faint murmur of tumult to be heard. The fires of battle were kindling, and the eyes of the world were turned upon the little green island across the Channel, and away from a nation who, to speak the truth, had been for some time relegated to the pages of our lesser comic magazines.

When Austria sent her ultimatum to Serbia there was still—except perhaps amongst the few who knew—only the vaguest interest taken in the impossible terms dictated by a great Power to a small one. We had scattered from towns, where things are discussed, to holiday places, where journalism is lazily criticized and generally believed to be untrue. Besides this, everything that was happening was happening in distant countries, while Ireland and the Ulster crisis were near at hand.

When the sound of the tumult actually attracted our attention, the hand that loves to hurl thunderbolts was already on our neighbour's door.

Much ink has been spilt in explaining why we went to war with Germany. Many learned treatises have been written on the diplomatic situation, and on the moral conditions that lie behind diplomacy. Almost everybody who is worth hearing has given his or her views, and those who are worth reading have written them. Almost it seems as if the last word had been said and the last criticism uttered. Men and women of every creed and of every race have expressed their sentiments about this war and about all wars since that day in August which made war inevitable. Probably a schoolboy, briefly and simply, might be able to put the matter as concisely as anyone else, and his creed, for all its simplicity, is a national one: "When you see a little chap being downed by a big one you cut in as soon as you can. And if the big bully says it's your turn

4

next and begins to swing his arms about, you take him on for all you're worth."

England has never allowed her friends to be bullied, and no one who knew her dreamed that she was going to allow it now. Her children—unexpectedly for those who did not know her—began to stop quarrelling with each other, and buckled on their swords to meet the common foe.

We were not ready—we did not pretend to be ready—but we meant to fight whether we were ready or not. Also, we meant to go on fighting till the end. The schoolboy's simple creed resolved itself into action. War had been declared; the thing which we had talked of for years had happened; and with the lifting of the veil of that peace which concealed the hate behind it, Germany stood revealed as England's old and implacable enemy. The revelation that we have been hated is always rather contemptible than enraging; and to our everlasting credit let it be said that England went to war with no notion of reprisals in her mind, and that only the subsequent dishonourableness with which she and her allies were treated even suggested reprisals. The war was a matter of national honour, and we went out to fight like gentlemen. We had a small army and not enough ammunition or rifles, and we had listened quite lately to politicians who, like mean folk at bargain counters, had demanded "still further reductions," and we went into the business as hopefully as usual, while in our heart of hearts the person we felt sorry for was the Kaiser.

Certainly he was sweeping through Belgium in a noisy vulgar way, trampling on everything that was beautiful, throwing down and hurting, killing and destroying, wantonly and odiously.

But "the little chap" with his back to the wall and his face set was putting up a fight, was contesting every inch of the ground that he still held, and was daily losing it by inches.

It is admitted, I suppose, on all sides, that we were unprepared. But we meant to "get one in," and with every echoing crash of falling cathedrals and beautiful buildings that we heard from the other side our determination and our indignation increased. It was crudely

5

expressed, of course; England is a plain-spoken body with a very poor power of self-expression. She can only sing, "It's a long way to Tipperary," when she goes out to die, and her war poems have sometimes made one smile.

But the spirit was there all the same, and a nation of shopkeepers keeps tucked away on her topmost shelves a good deal of sentiment, which is only brought down on very rare occasions. When it appears it generally surprises customers, who up till then had no idea that such a commodity was kept on the premises.

The shop people and the manufacturers, and the men who dig coal out of mines, and the men who stick pins into the lapels of their coats and measure out ribbons and speak of things being sweetly pretty, met each other unexpectedly in the trenches afterwards, and it was good for them to meet.

Meanwhile, older men were informing the world generally that they had better just wait a little! Why, "seventeen of our lads" had gone from the office or the counter, and this was going to mean trouble for Kaiser Bill [Wilhelm II, the last German Emperor and King of Prussia]. Belgian forts might be falling, towns sacked, cathedrals destroyed; we still pointed to maps with little flags stuck into them, and explained that "Bill" was in a tight place, and we thought it too!

It was foolish because at the moment it was not true, but it was fine because we meant it should be true some day; and if "seventeen of our lads" never came back, and many times seventeen times seven had still to go, we felt big enough for the job in front of us, and to feel big enough for the job in front is practically everything.

We sent our little army out, and began to manufacture a big one. We manufactured it quietly and quickly, and without much ostentation. The nation of shopkeepers took down from their topmost shelves the boxes labelled "Sentiment," which had grown very dusty for a while, and we realized what we had always known before, that the contents of the boxes were not saleable, but were given with both hands and ungrudgingly. "The lads" began to learn the art of putting on puttees in spirals round their legs, and took off

6

the black coats with the white pins stuck in the lapels, and gave up Saturday afternoon bicycle rides with their best girls. Thus a new army began to be made.

It was not too soon. There was a soldier living at Ascot then, a small soldier eighty years of age, an upright and God-fearing man, with eyes which had seen many things and saw far-one who had not unloosed the sandals from his feet nor untied his shoe-strings when his marching days were over, but had "slogged it," as soldiers say, from one place to another in England, calling for an army, passionately demanding fighting men. But we were busy over strikes and appeals for higher wages, and money-getting; and we were rather smug too, and did not want to be disturbed. So, while we admired the old soldier's energy, and gave him a hearing, because we are always glad to hear good speakers, his appeal failed every time. We were all right. Some one had said that we might sleep comfortably in our beds, and the soothing phrase had caught on, as the saying goes. It was a much more agreeable prophecy than the one the soldier was preaching; and, grown lazy in our comfortable security, we took the pleasant advice that was offered to us, and slept. England had neither sufficient rifles nor sufficient men when the war broke out, and "Bobs " never once said, "I told you so."

I like to think that almost the last thing I did before I left England was to motor down to have lunch at Ascot with Lord Roberts [Field Marshal Frederick Sleigh Roberts, one of the most successful commanders of the 19th century], and to bid him good-bye. He was full of news of the war, and in so far as it was possible he talked simply and openly about it, without that almost overdone discretion with which those who are privileged to have near information about things often do talk, and I was struck anew by the fact that a man who had been in the thick of so many fights was full of tenderness towards the suffering which war brings. His mind seemed filled with distress and indignation at the cruelty of the German method of warfare. He said: "I have fought in the Indian Mutiny [known in India as the Sepoy Rebellion], and against Afghans, and Zulus, and Kafirs, and Hill tribes, but none of these have ever committed such deeds of savagery as the Germans have done." We were hearing of

7

Louvain then, and of Liege, and of Lille and Namur, and we were almost near enough to stricken Belgium to catch the echo of women's cries and the shrieks of young girls; we were near enough to know all about the unarmed helpless people who were not spared by the soldiers in the gray coats. Afterwards, the saddest experience that I had in the war was to see the undeserved suffering of non-combatants, and I know nothing more heartrending than to find old women with their white hair stained with blood, or little toddling creatures wounded by shells. Lord Roberts believed that German barbarism was a byword amongst civilized people. For myself, I think we may forget all about it, for our memories are proverbially short; but I do not think Belgium ever will forget, and France will never forgive.

Lord Roberts told me that he meant to go to the front even if he could get no farther than Ostend; and he seemed to brush aside his years and his declining health as if no consideration could have any weight when there was work to be done. He reached the front, as we know, and he died there [November 14, 1914]. And so this war became another of his victories—his last, and perhaps the greatest of all....

Many people returned to London in the month of August, for there was an impatient longing to be near the centre of things. Also, committees sprang up like mushrooms in a night, and must be attended. The need for action made itself felt everywhere and in many different ways, and energy was expressed by "inquiries" everywhere. My own Red Cross Corps summoned its members to return to London. It was called "mobilizing at head-quarters"—for we were all inclined towards military terms in those days—and I used to find that by wearing a red cross, one was immediately believed to be a sort of peripatetic bureau of information. From searching questions as to how to make a shirt, up to the general and most pressing needs of the British Army, I was appealed to for directions, while the British Red Cross Society at Devonshire House was beset by persons in search of information of the same sort.

Women were, I think, exceptionally military in those days. It sometimes took the form of wearing a soldier's greatcoat, rather large and heavy, thrown open, and with a belt at the back and a good deal of material about it. Uniforms became a necessity, but more important even than uniforms were badges. One could hardly knit a pair of khaki socks without a brassade on one's left arm, and work became easier if accompanied by a stamped metal button. Everyone was making "calls to women," and the women responded by calling at bureaux, and were frequently snubbed, which left them wondering why they had been called. It was in those days that one first heard people humming the soldiers' song which one now hears all over Belgium, but which, as a battle slogan, has always seemed to me a little thin.

At music halls and *revues,* girls, dressed as admirals and colonels, saluted with alarming sharpness all the time.

War "wasn't such a bad thing" then: it was going to do every one good and brace every one up, and the man in the street, watching some regiment march away, began to talk of armies who would be " wiped out " in three weeks or so. Meanwhile, the women bought badges and the men expensive kits. Both became very shabby before very long, and both took their proper place in the scheme of things in *le bon Dieu' s* good time. But London stamped her name on preparations at first, and buttons and things in leather cases were important. Alas! they have strewn many a battlefield since then; and the field-glasses which we gave our boys have been left in muddy trenches or given to some comrade after poor So-and-so was gone, and all the smart straps and buckles have got dim with hard usage. But the buttons and the badges have helped to keep men's and women's spirits up, and just as we used to fight for a rag of bunting, so now we are content to die for the sake of some brass letters on the shoulder straps of our coats.

It was when the boys' new uniforms began to arrive, and they tried on flat caps in front of the mirror in the drawing-room, and buckled on bright swords which were expensive and beautiful, that we began to feel, not how dear, but just how young they were! We did not pretend it was not heart-breaking. All the dearest ones were soldiers and sailors, as they ought to be, but would this world be much fun without them, just suppose.... Besides, their mothers were crying.

9

Mr. Punch, God bless him! was our best consoler in those days, just as he has been our comforter and friend in many distant lands, and in many rough and lonely places ever since we knew him. Mr. Punch found the soul of the war, and acknowledged the bleeding price of it, and he showed pictures of things as they were in Belgium and in France, where already the fields were strewn with dead, and the blood of their children cried from the ground. And he showed us a man standing bareheaded beside his flag, and defying his enemy to make him or his country lose their souls whatever else might be lost. He told us not to give men and boys drink because it made them feel ashamed the next morning; and he told them also, gravely at first, what they were fighting for and why. And then he began, in his inimitable way, to have same fun with them, and to tell the soldiers in the trenches that the man with the big moustaches was a theatrical humbug, and that Uhlans were heavy swells, and he snapped his brave old fingers at both! He did not refer again to burning villages and murdered women, because, like the wise old boy he is, he never rubs things in; but he gave us some jokes which men under fire had made, and he laughed at raw recruits and made funny verses about them, although half the time his heart was almost breaking. He was always on the right note—never discordant and always a gentleman, not flippant, but with the same old grin for every one; and let it be remembered that Mr. Punch is a hunchback, and can still grin, and that, like many other non-combatants, he is fighting every inch of the way.

We, for our part, were "military," and bandaged little messenger boys with the rest. We talked about "rashions" and "revellies," and we " fell in " frequently, because nothing makes a section leader so happy or so surely a soldier as saying " Fall in!" and we had a drumhead service, and marched (rather badly, I am afraid) through London, but the Sunday crowds cheered us, and I do believe we all felt like doing our bit.

Often afterwards, when wounded and dying men were lying thick on a field-hospital floor, and the ambulances were bringing in their ghastly burdens from the field, and when there was hardly time even to remove the dead from amongst the dying, I used to think of the drill and the white-capped stretcher-bearers at home, and the little messenger boys with their innocuous wounds, which were so neatly and laboriously dressed.

The messenger boys' wounds were always conveniently placed, and they never screamed and writhed or prayed for morphia when they were being bandaged. And shoulders were not shot away, nor eyes blinded, nor men's faces—well, not much good ever came of talking of the things one has seen, and they are best left undescribed. "These are not wounds, they are mush," I heard one surgeon say; and then I thought of the little messenger boys and their convenient fractures.

One day in London, as I walked back after drill, across the park, I met an old friend of mine, who told me that Mrs. Stobart was taking out a women's unit to Belgium, and she suggested that I should join her. Mrs. Stobart herself seconded the suggestion, and I went on to the committee that was then formed, and we began to have hot little meetings in rather a small room. It was all somewhat fatiguing, I remember, and there were a great many delays about passports and the like; and we interviewed a large number of voluntary workers, who spoke of "Atthefront" as if it was one word, and who all said they were strong and did not mind what they did. We chose our staff in what must have appeared to be rather a haphazard fashion. But the average of humanity is good, and, on the average, is seldom disappointing.

Mrs. Stobart left for Brussels to establish her hospital there; but Brussels fell, and she was taken prisoner, and that caused a delay. We continued to sit in the small room and to talk, and no doubt, like many others, we justified our reputation as a women's committee by finding each other a little lacking in intelligence, and not always successfully concealing the fact.

We were all, I think, glad to get off on the 20th September. Our many attempts at starting had often resulted in disappointment, and we had begun to say "red tape" with a snort of indignation. We all said "red tape" in those days whenever things were delayed or did not go to our liking—it was another name for opposition. We also talked of the War Office as being "hidebound." It did us good, and it did no one else much harm.

At last we got off.

It was Sunday when we started, and one was struck by the fact that the whole of the months of August and September had been very like a Sunday in London. I have never seen so little traffic in the streets, and except for the marching regiments one saw but little stir. England, we learned, "had not quite realized the war yet." One forgave the expression then, because it takes a little while to get anything into English people's dear slow heads. But afterwards— when every man was wanted and some did not come—the old excuse began to get a little bit loose in the glue. To lend a hand should be an instinct surely. And to our credit be it said that it has been an instinct on which we have acted throughout the whole of our national life.

One likes the answer of the wee Scottish recruit, who, when asked if he had enlisted, replied, " Ay, I thocht it was time: yon Kaiser is goin' ower far." Or the gentleman, recorded in the pages of *Punch,* who, when he was refused at the recruiting station because of his age or his size, replied in a rage, "All right, only don't blame me if you lose this war.

Each of these men felt the whole responsibility of England on his own shoulders. It is the only way in which to join the army.

I remember a long wait at the railway station when we were leaving London for Tilbury, and I remember also that I forgot my passport and sent my maid, who had come to see me off, flying back for it in a taxi, and I also remember hoping sincerely that no one in the corps would hear anything about it. My official title was Head of the Orderlies, and for a head orderly to forget her passport would doubtless sound rather bad! However, a more truly cordial lot of people it would be difficult to find than our unit turned out to be. The passport was successfully retrieved, and we set sail.

It was one of those voyages which produce the deeply-sworn "never again" of suffering passengers. One regretted living on an island. One was willing to vote millions for a Channel tunnel, and the only comforting verse of Scripture that suggested itself for one's tombstone was "There shall be no more sea." One promised oneself one more voyage only, as long as life lasted, and that was back to England again.

At Antwerp we were met by carriages sent for us by the British Consulate, and, feeling empty, we put on the Patent Patriotic Smile, which we believed to be suitable for "the Front." The Patent Patriotic Smile helped afterwards, and it was just as well to begin to practise it, even though one was still feeling very seasick.

There was a great deal to do. The medical stores and part of the luggage were taken out of the boat, and we drove to the "Harmonie," where we found a large summer concert-hall placed at our disposal as a hospital. It was an ideal building, except, of course, as a protection against shell-fire. The high ceiling and the many windows gave plenty of light and ventilation, and the whole place had a bright and friendly air. The good nuns at the convent opposite gave us sleeping accommodation and a dining-room, while a few bedrooms were available for surgeons and orderlies in the hospital itself. We began to put up beds, and to allot to each person her special post. The girls, of course, and very naturally, were all keen about ward work. No one had come out to Antwerp to wait on or cook for an English staff, for instance. They must serve soldiers! There was a determined competition for heavy work, while not many "H.M.S. Helpfuls," as certain of my young friends have now named fussy workers, were present. I have always felt that zeal has a right to expend itself like any other form of energy, and that it can be expended wholesomely if it has an outlet, while assuredly it will not make for peace if that outlet is denied it. It should, I believe, be given a wide scope in the matter of work, even if it takes the curious form of a jealous passion for sweeping out a ward with a long-handled broom.

In a few days there was not so much anxiety to claim the whole share of every one's work on the part of our staff as there was at the outset, and they began to settle down into their stride in a very commendable spirit. The wounded had begun to arrive almost before our 130 beds were in order, but at first the cases were not so serious as those which afterwards came to us. Free from anxiety, and with patients doing well, the time passed pleasantly. The authorities gave the hospital unstinted praise, and we were visited by various personages of high position. We liked the Belgians, and I believe they liked us, and in the delightful garden of the "Harmonie" we made many friends. Of course, we had our favourites amongst the patients—Alfred, whose bed was always surrounded because he spoke English; and Sunny Jim, who had, on some pretext or another, remained in the hospital until long after he was quite well; and a few English soldiers who wrote post cards, and convalescents in red flannel jackets, who sat on benches in the sun and smoked. A not too rigorous routine was established, and we found ourselves very well content with Antwerp, and talked of passing a considerable time there.

CHAPTER II.

ANTWERP.

As every one now knows, the life of the hospital was very brief, but while it lasted it was very satisfactory. I believe many wounded soldiers will remember with pleasure the big airy concert-hall and the pleasant garden which surrounded it. The hall and the garden always had a certain air of gaiety about them, in curious contrast to their present uses; but this was good for the men who had looked on far other sights not many miles away. Under the trees were groups of chairs and marble tables, reminiscent of "refreshments" and an open-air social life. The tables formed ward-tables afterwards; and in the wide, sunny balcony of the hospital the rows of chairs were always in use by convalescents, who used to shiver in the sunbeams, delicate still, and with horny hands rolled up dry tobacco in cigarette papers.

We must have been singularly fortunate in our patients, or else, as I shrewdly suspect, the Belgians are naturally good mannered. Their gratitude was shown in a thousand ways; but I believe nothing gave the hospital staff more pleasure than when it took the form of presenting Mrs. Stobart with a couple of handsome bronze medals in a case. She herself was much touched by this gift, and made a nice speech in return for it. Our patients seemed to consider that when they said, "Je suis tres content de rester ici," they might remain in the hospital as long as they liked; and indeed we should have been contented ourselves to have had them remain.

We grew fond of the patient, quiet, small men, who, even when they were in pain, were always grateful and always polite, and who seemed to have a genuine enthusiasm for England. Their "Thank you verra moch" was always spoken in English, out of compliment to their allies, I believe!

One wishes the pleasant useful time could have lasted longer. According to the newspapers, it was going to last indefinitely. And every day we read in the journals, "pour le reste, tout est calme" in Antwerp, while if one's own ears were to be believed, the sound of firing seemed to get nearer every day. We used to amuse ourselves at breakfast-time by asking for newspaper accounts of what was happening, and contrasting them with what we saw for ourselves, until at last even the newspapers admitted that the forts were "threatened."

I took a little carriage one afternoon and drove to the second line of fortifications. In Belgium, which is the muddiest country in the world, and where water lies long on the level roads, there is always a slightly raised track of stones in the middle of the streets, with a slough of mud on either side of it. Subsequently, one knew these roadways well, and got accustomed to the sudden dives which motor cars and ambulances took when passing each other on the narrow ways; but at first one was puzzled to find oneself driving on cobbles right out into the country.

My knowledge of military matters is small indeed, and my knowledge of fortifications and constructions is even less; yet I must confess to a feeling of surprise—for which I offer excuses to those who know much better than myself—when I saw the forts. I had always heard that Antwerp was one of the best-protected towns in the world, and, indeed, I had often heard it called impregnable; but the grass-grown ramparts and the old stone-built forts looked to my ignorant eyes like remnants of medievalism: it was impossible to think of them as being designed to stand a heavy siege of modern artillery; indeed, the impression that was conveyed to the mind was that of some slumbering old fortification, such as one is often taken to see because of its historic interest. I passed fields in which me were laboriously placing wooden stakes which they told me, were put there to lame horses. And there seemed to linger about Antwerp a notion of cavalry charges up to the walls of the city. Even the wire entanglements looked like mere playthings, and quite unfit to stop hosts of marching men. Antwerp was shelled from six miles away! The wooden pegs, which looked as if some gardener was preparing to plant a field with bulbs, could be avoided by making a detour of one hundred yards on either side of them; and the wire entanglements no doubt were subsequently pulled up with one hand, and could hardly, it seemed to me, have stopped a regiment of schoolgirls armed with bonnet-pins.

I never saw the outer forts, but I enjoyed a survey of the inner ones, in much the same way in which one enjoys seeing oubliettes and drawbridges and loopholes for arrows, and other interesting remnants of a bygone system of defence. Cavalry advancing by road and through a ploughed field might have found Antwerp an awkward place to negotiate; otherwise I could not discover what the defences were for.

A few lines of trees had been cut down, while others had been spared, and a great many small gardens had been trampled out of existence, in preparation for an assault by 16-inch guns! The place seemed to my ignorant mind to be doomed beforehand, and no doubt that doom was hastened by treachery within the walls. A large German population is not easily or immediately sorted out at a crisis, and the fall of Antwerp, which took so many persons by surprise, could hardly, I think, have been unanticipated by those who were in the city.

On the 25th we began to hear the sound of guns, and one afternoon a Taube [a pre-World War I monoplane aircraft] flew overhead. One grew well accustomed to the visit of these destructive birds in the weeks that followed, but this was the first one I had seen. They are singularly graceful in their flight, and it is difficult to connect their dove-like sailing overhead with dropped bombs and "silent death" and destruction.

Our guns fired at the one which sailed over the hospital, and there was some little commotion in the street outside; while a piece of shrapnel fell through the roof of our hospital and considerably startled a wounded man beside whose bed it landed. The bursting shells looked like bits of cotton wool in the sky, and amongst them the Taube sailed away again, having had a look at us and laid an egg very rudely in our midst.

The firing could constantly be heard after this, and the work of the hospital became very heavy. Two orderlies always took turns in sitting up at night so as to be able to give a helping hand to the

17

nurses and doctors, who were kept busy day and night. The bell at the street gate used to ring, and we knew that one vehicle, moving more slowly than the others that tore up and down the road, contained wounded men slung on stretchers behind the canvas tilt of the ambulance. Our work had developed into routine very quickly. We used to go down the long passage to the gateway, where a little crowd with a taste for horrors always assembled to see what could be seen, and here we received the different cases and took their names and regimental numbers before handing them over to the surgeons. Later, clothes had to be sorted and labelled, and sent to be disinfected and cleaned; and it became a work of some magnitude to empty the men's pockets of their various treasures, and label and number them and put them away. The Belgian loves his small possessions, and carries about with him the most curious collection of things; and in his knapsack, whose principal merit might seem to be that it should be light, he often carries presents for all his family; and I have frequently been called upon to admire the silk scarves, the baby's shoes, and the bottles of scent which they contained.

In their greatcoats we used to find loaded revolvers side by side with sardine tins and candle ends and oddments of every description. They were all very pockety, and many of them were not of the sort that can be conveniently baked in a furnace; but I think we loyally looked after them all, and each patient got his queer goods when he was discharged.

We used to serve oxo [presumably she means oxygen] to the men as soon as they were brought in, and we had hot water bottles ready for them. The worst of it all was that everything had to be done in the dark. Orders were compulsory about lights being turned out by eight o'clock, and after that hour a good deal of groping used to begin, and marble tables with unsuspected legs were frequently overturned with a crash. We used to hold electric torches for the doctors who were dressing wounds, and I think I have never seen such exhaustion as the soldiers showed. They often went to sleep while the bandages were being placed upon them, and I have even seen a man doze heavily while a cut in his forehead was being stitched.

The darkness and the want of water were the two baffling things about that time in Antwerp; and indeed the groping about, when the short days closed in, was one of the worst things about the whole winter. The Germans destroyed the reservoir near Antwerp, and all the water for the hospital and for our own men had to be fetched in buckets from a neighbouring well. We used to go out after supper, offering to carry things for each other as women will, and fill every available receptacle and carry them back to the two houses before going to bed.

About this time we got orders to evacuate the wounded; but later, when all the patients who could move were dressed, we were begged to remain and to keep the hospital open. The authorities told us frankly that the town would without doubt be bombarded, and that the Government, etc., were leaving; also that any of the hospital unit who wanted to return home were at liberty to do so. Only one or two took advantage of the permission, and the rest remained.

There was a certain sense of strain about the days that followed. The weather was still and quiet, and the autumn leaves dropped plentifully in the convent's peaceful garden where we lodged, while the booming of guns went on all the time, and every one began to leave the city.

The Government officials and the Consulate departed for England, and every boat was packed with crowds of refugees of all classes. There was no panic, but certainly a very fixed determination to get away. Meanwhile, we still read "Tout est calme;" and I suppose that when a town is nearly emptied of its inhabitants it has rather a calm appearance. We might ourselves have imagined that all was calm had it not been for the frequently arriving ambulances at the door. Each case seemed more pitiful than the last, and at night time especially it was heartbreaking to hear the cries in the wards. From a distance, I fancy that the actual suffering that war brings is sometimes not appreciated, or may even be overlooked. It is not, perhaps, well to insist upon it, but a hospital at the front leaves nothing unrealized in this respect. And still the news from the trenches was bad. Even English soldiers and sailors said it was bad; and when English soldiers and sailors admit that they are not winning hands down, one may begin to suspect that the outlook is serious.

I often went to the gate of the garden to see the ceaseless stream of motor conveyances tearing up and down between our hospital and the trenches. The stream never ceased, and the hooting of horns never ceased, while the sense of hurry and stress went on all the time. When the cars were English, the occupants would often stop to ask the way at the crossroads; and to one's question, "What news?" there would come a shake of the head and, "Not very good."

We all spent most of our days in the wards then, and got Belgian women to do the other work. At night time the concert-hall, with its platform and gay pillars and the forgotten air of gaiety about it, always struck me as being particularly sad. It seemed like a living protest against the destruction of simple happiness in a big provincial town, where men and women had enjoyed music, and tea at little marble tables, and a concert-hall with singers in it. Now it was plunged in darkness, and nurses with tiny lights, going up and down between the straight little beds, had to listen to cries of "A boire, mademoiselle," all through the night. They moved about softly with their little torches and straightened a pillow here and there, while overhead was a great arch of decorated ceiling, all gay with painted flowers. Wounded men coming in out of the dark used to blink oddly at the concert-hall and at the nurses and doctors; but I used to think they did not question anything or think of anything much except their own suffering. I had had an idea that I should be kept busy writing letters for them, or sending messages to their homes, but a good many of the poor fellows were too ill for this; and as time went on, our hospital being nearest to the actual fighting, we used to receive cases all night long.

The guns were now so close that the air used to shake with them; and, alas! we had to refuse many patients owing to want of room. On Sunday, the 3rd, however, we were quite sure that all would now be well, for some London omnibuses had arrived, and it was quite impossible to associate a respectable London omnibus with defeat!

20

They still had advertisements on them, redolent of familiar streets, and were filled with naval men. We admitted that we were "thrilled," and we went to the gate to wish them "good luck" as they passed, and to tell them to come to us to be nursed if they were wounded. In more emotional days the feeling of safety which our countrymen gave us might have excused expressions of sentiment; as it was, we were "cheery," according to the fashion of our day, and according to the fashion of the hospital, where the meals were always of a lively description. We gave the men the best "send off" that was possible, and they shook hands with us and said, "We will take care of you, sister." In our minds there was a sense of relief; for there is no doubt about it, omnibuses and sailors do give a great sense of security!

It is far too early to speak of the diplomatic side of the war, or to venture on criticism. The arrival of the Naval Brigade did not prevent the fall of Antwerp. And let us leave it at that.

The hurrying motor cars and ammunition vans began to go more swiftly up and down the road, and now we noticed that many of them were damaged. The men who were driving them showed us great lumps of shell which they had picked up on the roadway, or would point to disabled engines and broken wings, and say, in answer to our exclamation, "It would have been a lot worse if that piece had fallen on my 'ead." They seemed sorry not to be able to give us a better account of how things were going; and when they got the chance they always ate largely and stolidly, and wiped their mouths, said "Good morning," and went into the firing-line again. They would not have parted with an old beloved pipe in those days for a ransom, and, like most soldiers and sailors, they could grumble about the want of sugar in their coffee, and then lay down their lives without a murmur.

CHAPTER III.

ANTWERP.

THE bombardment began on the 7th of October at midnight. One does not wish to include unnecessary personal narrative in an *October* account of work at the front, but the first sound of shells is unexpected and a *1914* little startling. Some people have described the noise as being a scream, and others have called it a yell, and we get such expressions as "whizzing" and "whistling," but I do not think any of these words quite describe it. It is a curious sound of rending, increasing in violence as the missile comes towards one, and giving one plenty of time to wonder, if one feels so disposed, whether it intends to hit one or not. This has its useful side if one is inclined to take cover, but it certainly adds a little to the mental discomfort which being under a prolonged bombardment involves. I slept in a small room—the museum of the convent school—with a large window in it. When the first shell arrived in Antwerp it came past my open window and fell quite close to the convent. So then we began to dress ourselves and, looking rather like a girls' school, I thought, we walked over in the bright moonlight to the hospital on the other side of the road. I suppose it was a matter of honour with us all not to walk quickly. There is a British obstinacy, of which one saw a good deal during the war, which refuses to hurry for a beastly German shell! It has cost a good many lives, but it is good all the same.

We found the hospital staff already very busy. As soon as the shells began to come over, the helpless wounded all began to scream, while some of those who, we imagined, would not walk again leapt out of bed. The nurses quieted everybody, and an assurance that we did not mean to desert them seemed to bring a curious sense of safety to the men—as if a handful of women could protect them from bursting shells!

The hospital, as I have said, was a lightly built structure, mostly made of glass, and underneath it was a small coke cellar. I do not fancy it gave any protection whatever, and there was always the chance that the building above might collapse and fall on the top of us, preventing our getting out, but that was one of the chances which had to be accepted, and the fact of being in any sort of cellar had a certain pretension of safety about it which satisfied the men.

On the day previous, we had done what we could in the way of removing iron gratings and bars which might choke the entrance to the little cellar; also we had arranged mattresses in it and stocked it with some provisions and plenty of water. Every one had been instructed where to find it, so there was no confusion. Our staff consisted solely of women: two girls went out and turned off the gas at the main, to prevent an explosion if we should be hit, and the others worked at the stretchers, carrying men from the hospital above into the small space below. I saw one little red-haired nurse carry three men in succession on her back down the little coal-shoot which formed the cellar's entrance!

Meanwhile the shells were "coming pretty thick," as a wounded English sergeant said.

Our orders were that everything was to go on as usual, and we were asked who was on night duty. We said good-night to those who were returning to the convent opposite, and the rest of us lighted little night-lights and stayed with the wounded. There were over a hundred of them in the cellar, but we had mattresses for the worst cases, and we went to the hospital above for extra pillows and blankets and to see that every bed was evacuated.

Most of the men slept, as soldiers seem able to do under any circumstances; but we had various distressing cases of painful gangrenous wounds and sickness, and these got no rest all night. Also, there were some disabled men who stood upright all the time, because the position was easier for them; and still others who slept on the little piles of coke that remained in the cellar. The small flames of the night-lights threw curious shadows on the groups of soldiers in their greatcoats and with heads or arms bound up, and on the white faces of those who lay on the mattresses.

I think the men liked having us with them, and they seemed to think it was civil of us women not to leave them, for I heard one man say to another, as he rolled round on his blanket on the floor, "Mon Dieu! que les Anglaises sont comme it faut!"

It "bucked one," as schoolboys say, to hear one's country well-spoken of. But indeed I believe a friendship has been established between us and Belgium which will not lightly be broken.

The night in the cellar seemed long; there was a constant noise of shivering glass as the impact of the shells destroyed our poor hospital, and we were anxious about our friends in the convent, for one shell certainly, crashing through masonry, sounded as though it must have seriously damaged the building. We looked at each other and said, "That's the convent gone!" But as a matter of fact it was the house next it which had been struck, and this was soon in flames. The convent itself had only a bit of its cornice taken off and some shutters damaged. We ourselves came in for rather more than our fair share of attention, I fancy, for we were (it was explained to me) on a line with the arsenal, against which fire was being directed. Be that as it may, the morning showed us much damage done—trees split up in the garden, and a hole six feet deep, where some nurses had laid some washing out to dry in front of the hospital.

The wounded English sergeant told us that firing would probably cease about dawn, because the enemy always liked to keep their guns concealed. Consequently, dawn was pretty welcome that morning. But the shelling was heavier than ever!

At six o'clock the "girls' school" walked over from the convent again, and very calmly began to prepare breakfast. I must confess that had some of the younger girls shown faintness or fear I should not, for one, have blamed them; but I did not see anyone give way even for a short time. I remember catching a friend's eye when a shell came very close to us, and so unpleasant was it, that we both began to laugh.

The nurses were bright and lively all the time, and chatted all through the night, and the wants of the sick and wounded kept most of us busy.

We could, I admit, have done with less firing when the men began to quit the hospital after breakfast. A military order came that all those who could walk were to leave; so they set out, and that was a pathetic and ghastly business. For they had not even crutches or sticks; but we cut up old boxes for them and, leaning on little bits of board, doubled up with pain and holding on to their comrades, they limped off down the long empty road, with "Jack Johnsons" still whizzing overhead [a heavy, black German 15-cm artillery shell; a reference to the African-American heavyweight boxing champion of the same name].

But only a small part of our difficulties was over when all the men who could limp or crawl had left us, for not only were we filled with anxiety as to what would become of them on their slow and painful journey to places of shelter, but we still had to determine how the "intransportables" could best be looked after and cared for. It was, of course, impossible that they should remain in the cellar or in the hospital. Already the latter place was partially wrecked, and it remained unsafe until (I am informed) it was hit by a shell and took fire just after we left it.

Three of our party started off to the town to see what they could arrange in the way of transport, while a young girl, whom we called the Transport Orderly, went unobserved and stood by the gate at a time when shells were flying "pretty thick," and remained there for an hour in the hope of seeing some empty vehicle coming back from the trenches which would take our poor wounded away. She informed me afterwards that she had " minded " for the first five minutes but not afterwards, and she seemed concerned that some soldiers had ducked behind a stone wall instead of "standing up to" the shells.

Either the right people were in Antwerp that day or else bombardments do not affect English nerves very much, or else, as I once heard a soldier say, "We are too well-bred to show it!" I have since always seen it stated that shells were bursting at the rate of four per minute, and although I cannot vouch for this statement, I do know that the noise never stopped for a moment all day and all night, and it was officially stated that many thousands of shells fell in the town. In the midst of it a few straggling soldiers sheltered where they could, while some of our little party, walking for three

25

hours in the deserted streets, found an Englishman who had discovered an entrance into a tuck-shop and was buying a German sausage, and taking great care to cut it into neat slices! At the field hospital the patients were having breakfast in the open air, after two shells had fallen into the courtyard; and nurses, questioned afterwards as to whether they felt frightened or not, always replied, "Oh no, much too busy!"

I was interested to discover from the various remarks I heard on the subject what was the motive—or perhaps one ought to say the sustaining power—behind the unfailing pluck which I saw on all sides. "Much too busy" was, as I have said, a common answer to the inquisitive questioner who wanted to know what were the exact sensations of being under shellfire. Others exclaimed, "I wasn't going to be frightened of Germans—rather not!" While there were those who merely remarked with dignity that they hoped they were ladies! And still others of thoughtful minds placed their confidence somewhat deeper. I was affected to observe that these latter were always to be relied on at all times and even under trying circumstances.

Our transport difficulty was not overcome, but it was certainly much relieved when our transport orderly who watched by the gate came in and said she had found a motor wagon, driven by a British soldier, who said he would help us to move our wounded. We filled it up with our worst cases and had them conveyed to a hospital in the town where there were excellent cellars, and then the transport wagon came back again and we loaded it once more with every man that could be packed into it. We sent two nurses in it also, and a surgeon and the ward interpreter; and the sole direction that it was possible to give them was to get out of the range of fire as soon as possible, and to send back some conveyance for us if they could do so.

After that we had a long wait. Nearly all the wounded had been dispatched, and there was not much to do. We sat in the convent kitchen and felt amazingly tired; also the noise of the bursting shells began to get rather maddening. At 5.30 we saw three English omnibuses coming back with ammunition from the trenches. The men who drove them offered to give us a lift if we would get in at once, and we did so. As soon as we were in the omnibus the spirits of all the girls rose with a bound. They climbed up on the roof, in order better to see the houses that were on fire all round us; they sang "Tipperary," and they lighted cigarettes in an omnibus filled with ammunition and petrol!

Most people, I think, believe themselves to have been the last to leave Antwerp. We ourselves got away about six o'clock, and the bridge was blown up a few hours later.

The scene down by the river was very striking. Some immense oil-tanks were in a blaze and lighted up the sky and the river and the town like some gorgeous sunset, while across the red sky the shells still flew.

Our omnibuses crossed the river in a ferry. I myself found the transit inconveniently slow, for the rumour was that fire was now being directed upon the shipping, and the crawling movement of the ferry hardly made motion perceptible; but I did not ask anyone else if they also would have preferred a little more speed.

When we reached the other side we set out to walk, with no fixed intention except to give as wide a berth as possible to the city of Antwerp. Before we had gone very far, however, some Belgian ambulances hove in sight, and these very kindly took us to the shelter of a convent at St. Gilles. The drive in the dark—for the dusk had now fallen—was full of vivid interest, for an endless stream of mounted soldiers and wagons lined the road. One heard the cracking of whips and the sound of horses' hoofs in the mud even when one could not see anything very clearly, and here and there were fires lighted under the trees, and some men cooking supper or sleeping—wherever they stopped, even for a few minutes, the men fell rather than lay down and slept.

We got into St. Gilles very late, and ate the small store of provisions we had been able to carry with us, and then the nuns gave us permission to sleep on the floor of one of their schoolrooms. We turned in (if that is an allowable expression for sleeping on a floor) about midnight, and at 3 a m. we had to get up again, the news being that "things were worse." But this was a scare, I fancy, and the order merely meant that we must get up and start immediately in the outgoing train for Ostend. We came away with some of the Naval Brigade, in the longest and slowest train I have ever been in. I was reminded of the old joke about the notice in a railway carriage in America, which said, "Passengers are forbidden to write their names on the telegraph posts when the train is in motion." When our train was not crawling it stopped altogether, and we used to get out and sit on the railway bank for a time, and then, as it jerked forward again, we would get back into carriages which smelt of sardines and tobacco.

I think I have never felt more strongly than I did on that long journey that an Englishman never knows when he is beaten. It seemed to me that whatever we might do in the future—and we all mean to "win in the end"—we were for the moment in the unhappy and horrible position of turning our backs on the enemy. I do not think the British who were our companions were downhearted or even conscious that they had had a reverse. Most of them in the third-class carriage in which I travelled were offering to bring me the Kaiser's head as a souvenir. Their minds ran on souvenirs, and they parted with buttons and bullets all the way down the line to villagers, who brought them apples and coffee. I did once meekly suggest to them that in order to get the Kaiser's head we ought to be travelling in the other direction; but this was a view of the matter which did not suggest itself to the Britisher. "It's all right, miss; if we don't get it for you to-day, you shall have it to-morrow." The Britisher was born cheery. Even when they were "gassed" they called out, "All right, Allemands, put another penny in the meter!"

We reached Ostend at midnight, having travelled since three o'clock in the morning, and found that every one in the place wanted to stop us and ask news of Antwerp. "Interviews" were demanded almost in the gutters, and our small party had to hasten on through the dark (for Ostend also was in a state of eclipse) to try to find accommodation. This, after many disappointments, we were able to do, and we were accorded the privilege of sleeping on the marble floor of a restaurant. It was not a particularly comfortable way of passing our third night out of bed; and the house for the moment could produce only three eggs and some bread for supper for our large party. I consider that it was very nearly a flight of genius on the part of one of us when it occurred to her to ask the *patronne* of the hotel whether the house could still produce some light champagne. It proved itself able to do so, and I was glad for the sake of the staff, who had worked so hard, that the evening ended in a manner that was determinedly gay. We were all nearly nodding with fatigue, but we drank our chief's health, and made the best we could out of a somewhat sorry occasion. It did not do to think of our hospital, with its beds and its comforts perhaps destroyed; and I was touched more than I like to say to hear the regrets of some of those who had lost all their small possessions in Antwerp.

During the day I had heard a good deal from the men in the train about the equipment which they had been obliged to leave behind them on the platform of the town we had quitted. They told me that each man's kit cost £6, and that they would have to be fitted out again when they went back to Folkestone. They got an immense reception there, which I, for one, do not grudge them; but women— the nurses and the orderlies and the staff—were adding up the value of the things that they had left behind, and I am sure no one ever knew when or where they landed in England! They came back unnoticed, and began to save up out of their little salaries money enough to replace their caps and aprons.

Still, we were able to wire home to our friends on the following morning that we were all right, and that was a certain satisfaction.

CHAPTER IV.

AT Ostend we found our little party of nurses and wounded men who had left us during the bombardment of Antwerp. One man had died, and many others were very ill. A small house had been given up 1914 to them, but it was quite evident that we should not long be able to remain at Ostend.

Our unit went back to England, and I was much struck to see the evidence of fatigue and strain on every one. More seasoned warriors than these women wore the stamp of the siege of Antwerp on their faces for a long time afterwards, and the "Antwerp look" passed into a sort of proverb [known today as the thousand-yard stare]. Our women had not slept for three nights; they had been under heavy shell-fire for eighteen hours (and they were new to shells in those days); and they were returning home after three weeks of exhausting work. But no one complained, and all were ready to stay on with the wounded. The only sign of strain which anyone showed was an inability to hear what was said. It took some time for a question to penetrate, and it was significant to hear how often every one said "What?"

I did not return to England, but waited at Ostend, which I found very interesting for a few days. There was something a little bit like a panic in the place, and so crowded were the boats going to England that people used to wait at the docks all night for early morning sailings. The crowds were quiet but anxious, and every one was on tip-toe to get away. One heard of people crossing in open boats. I do not know if this was true or not; but I saw the waiting crowds myself, and the wounded, and the men seemed terribly afraid of being taken prisoners.

The Germans were not far off, and it was a great bore clearing out in front of them again.

At Ostend I met Dr. Munro, retreating like the rest of us with his ambulances and his staff. He suggested I should join them, which I did; and on Tuesday, the 13th, after a confused breakfast, served in a hurry, we mounted the ambulances and went to Dunkirk [site of the famous evacuation in the next war]. The road was lined and filled with people, walking or in carts or carriages, all trying to get away. Everywhere we were asked for "lifts," and every one was carrying something. It was a stormy day of wind and rain, which added a great deal to the distressfulness of the scene.

At Dunkirk there was no room for any of us at any of the hotels, so we went out to Malo les Bains, which is the little seaside suburb of Dunkirk, approachable by tramway, and we commandeered there a little hotel which had been shut up for the winter. All the carpets were up, and Malo at that time suggested nothing to me but an empty bathing machine, so suggestive was the little place of summer visitors, all now fled and gone.

As far as I remember, the evening ended pleasantly on bacon and eggs, served by an excitable landlady with black hair.

I was interested to find the ladies of our corps with maps and motor cars. Most of them were good chauffeurs, and all were well posted up in war news. I heard a man in a responsible position say to a girl, "How far are we from the firing-line?" and she was able to inform him, of course. Later, I used to hear the same sort of appeals made constantly, "Have you been able to get our passports?" "Where are we to get petrol?" "Can you find us tyres?" "What is the password?"

Perhaps the ladies' superior knowledge of French gave me the idea that much of the organization and practical work, both of hospitals and ambulances in Belgium, were due to them. Later on I was struck by their pluck and their resourcefulness; but at Malo I first learned what good organizers they can be.

News was very scarce at first, but the newspapers, like some dear old hurdy-gurdy with only one tune to play, loyally drummed out tales of victories. The sound of firing was still audible, and I am interested to note that during nine months in Belgium there were not many days on which the boom of guns could not be heard either near or far away. When the firing was loud and heavy, it was our invariable custom to remark that those must be British guns. Of the German artillery we always spoke as if high explosives and heavy field-pieces were some happy chance fallen from heaven on that very undeserving people.

The "preparedness" of our cousins, who have declared friendship for us for so many years, and have had, so to speak, the run of the house, both here and in India, gave one much to ponder over and consider. Everywhere there was evidence that war had been intended for years past. In Belgium itself pretty, innocent-looking villas, inhabited by some stout German bourgeois, were found to be well provided with concrete floors for mounting guns, and even the carriage drives had been carefully prepared for the traffic of heavy ammunition vans. Artillery that had, perhaps, been sent to some local exhibition had been unaccountably left there, and was conveniently discovered when wanted, and no doubt Germany must often have smiled when some of our peace-loving politicians advised drastic economies in our army and navy.

Malo was such a serene little place that it was almost impossible to associate it with the thought of war. One saw a level sea and a few fishing boats going out with the tide. On the long gray shore shrimpers waded with their nets, and often the only colour on the beach was the little wink of white that the breaking waves made on the sand. The rows of empty bathing-boxes gave it the air of a theatre seen by daylight when the audience is no longer there; but it was evidently a place of simple amusements and friendly holiday times.

Damaged ambulances and cars coming in from the front seemed out of place at Malo. I remember seeing one that had been brought to the arsenal to be repaired. It had been a German one once, painted gray, and with the Prussian eagle upon it. This had been obuterated with a few streaks of colour to suggest the French *tricolor,* and mechanics were now repairing it. Its sides were literally riddled with bullet-holes, and its engine smashed. The man behind the wheel must have known something of what fighting means. He was killed, of course, and one realized that to sit behind a wheel with one car rapidly becoming like a sieve must require some nerve.

Speaking of Malo, one cannot do less than mention some of the excellent hospitals which were afterwards established there. The one which I personally saw most of belonged to Millicent, Duchess of Sutherland, and I cannot speak too highly of her work. A French soldier, who was wounded and taken there, told me afterwards of his experiences. He said the hospital was almost full when he arrived, and that it was proposed that the last available bed should be given to an officer, but "Madame la Duchesse" said, "No; a wounded man is a wounded man, and there is no distinction between them."

So the wounded soldier got the bed, and I never heard what became of the officer.

There was plenty of good work done by various people— sometimes by those of whom one least expected it. I remember, for instance, hearing some doubt expressed in the earlier stages of the war as to whether a barge with ladies, generally associated in the public mind with social life, would be of much service in distributing clothes and necessities to Belgian refugees. But no one who has seen them visiting in the poorest houses and pinning bundles of clothes together with their own hands, could for a moment doubt their usefulness. The work of these ladies, and of many others during the war, seemed to produce a favourable and most grateful expression of feeling on the part of the Belgians.

On the 22nd of October we moved out to Furnes. On the road there, one saw what one was afterwards to get so well accustomed to—an endless stream of motors and men. The motors were of every size and description, and everything on wheels had to carry what it could. A gray-lined, once sumptuous car would often be filled to the roof with loaves of bread, while a lumbering *carrion*, hooting noisily like everything else, would show an interior stacked with planks or petrol tins. One's previous notion of soldiers "marching as to war" may have been associated in one's mind with bands playing, and the stirring sound of marching feet. Here, one saw some tired men grimly slogging along, their uniforms covered with mud, and their boots often worn out. But every inch of Belgium was being contested by them! They were flying no banners, but they stuck to the trenches, and with one little corner of their country left to them, they held their own and fought stubbornly and obstinately.

Nothing was ready for us at Furnes, so we had to motor back to Malo to sleep, and we started again the next morning at 5 a m. The roads were nearly empty then, and I remember we made the journey in a Brooklands racing car, in which I was somewhat insecurely perched on some petrol tins. Our chauffeur said when we arrived that he had "knocked sixty miles an hour out of her." This may or may not have been true, but I do not ever remember travelling so fast before, and I could have done with a more secure seat than the one I was on.

When we reached the hospital we heard that fighting had been going on all night, and already the wounded were beginning to come in. We often spoke afterwards of the time that followed as the busiest we had ever known. It certainly was one which emphasized what is glibly spoken of as the horrors of war.

A large ecclesiastical college had been made over to the field hospital, and wards were not only already prepared, but were already filled. Our ambulances, together with those of the Belgians, brought in the wounded both by day and by night. Men and women drove these ambulances, and they were coming in ceaselessly all the time. The courtyard of the college was always filled with cars, and filled, too, with the sound of throbbing engines and clutches being jerked, and all the noises which arrival and departure involve. Stores were being unpacked, and one noticed how many people said, "Where?" and then hastened on without waiting for a reply. "Where is the chloroform?" "Where are the stretchers?" "Where are the Germans?" "Where (even) are the dead to be put?"

No one stopped to answer. The wounded continued to come in, and the guns were firing all the time. The first of the ambulances that had been out all night used to arrive about 10 a. m. carrying battered men on its pitiful shelves.

"Take care; there are two fearfully bad cases inside. Step together! The man on the top stretcher is dead, lift him down. Steady! Lift the others out first. Now, carry them across the yard to the overcrowded ward, and lay them on the floor, for all the beds are full. Lay them down, and go for others. Take the worst cases to the operating

34

theatre, and cut off the shattered limb. Here is a man in the ward just dead; lift him out, and make room for another."

All round the stoves on the floor the stretchers are lying closely packed. A hurrying nurse covers a man's face as she passes, and the *brancardiers* [stretcher bearer] carry him out. A doctor enters with disinfectants, and sprinkles the floor where he can, for nearly all of it is covered with stretchers. A half-starved boy with both his hands in bandages is unable to hold a spoon, and when he is fed with a bowl of porridge and milk, he stops before it is half finished and says, "I'm afraid there won't be enough for the others." A few cushions in the corner of the room are all that we can give him, and even these must be given up soon, for every man who can travel must go on to Calais or Dunkirk. The firing is pretty near now, and the wounded are coming in sometimes at the rate of a hundred a day.

A young friend of mine at home said to me, "I suppose, though, on the whole, you are having a very good time."

A French boy of sixteen dies very slowly and painfully; and children are brought in, and girls with their legs smashed, and old women with white hair are horribly wounded. These latter cases must go to the civil hospital. Only soldiers can remain in the field hospital. And there isn't nearly enough room for them!

It is about five o'clock in the afternoon, when the light fails, that the worst hour in the hospital begins. The dim lamps are lighted, and people begin to fall over things. Also, this is the hour, it seems to me, when men feel pain most, when the wounded in beds and on the floor begin to cry out. How they suffer! Here is a young boy with his eyes shot out; and several beds in a row contain men with head wounds, the result of bursting shrapnel overhead. And there are other cases far too pitiful to describe; and men who have lost their reason; and men moaning for morphia; and a baby of three years old with both his legs broken and a little bandaged hand at which he looks with wonder.

It isn't a good time. War is not a merry picnic.

35

Blood-covered mattresses and pillows are carried out into the courtyard. There is always a great pile of rags and bandages being burnt outside. A curious smell pervades everything.

In the midst of it all doctors and nurses keep their heads and are never flurried, never less than careful and attentive. They sit up all night, and in the noisy daytime get but little sleep; they have become inured to seeing death and suffering without being hardened by it, and their patience is admirable.

On an afternoon the Queen of the Belgians came to visit the hospital. It seemed to me then, as it seems to me now, that few things could so wring the heart of any woman as to visit the wounded of an army in the remnant of a kingdom as she did.

On the day she came, the wards were as full as usual, and she spoke to each man there. In the evening an old friend of my own appeared, coming in out of the darkness, in the unexpected way people do in war time, and we went round the wards together. Mme. Curie and her daughter were attached to the hospital for a time, and looked after the X-Rays, and some journalists came before the stringent rules were subsequently enforced that none were to be admitted.

There was heavy fighting at Dixmude [Diksmuide, West Flanders, Belgium] at that time, and one night was especially full of interest and of excitement. The town was being heavily shelled, and some of our ambulances went in to get the wounded. The account that some of these men gave afterwards of the scene which they witnessed was dramatic in the extreme. One friend of mine told me that Dixmude was like some city which a man might see in a drunken dream. Houses were falling, and buildings were literally reeling as the shells struck them; spires had been knocked crooked, and it hardly seemed possible that anything could remain alive through that night. As far as I can remember, eight men of our corps went in on ambulances when the shelling was at its worst to fetch the wounded out of the cellars where they had been laid.

A son of the Belgian War Minister was with us in those days, and he it was who saw to the loading up of the ambulances, and who gave orders for them to start. When all were full, the chauffeur on the last ambulance believed that the order had been given for him also to start, and it was not until the three heavily laden vehicles were a considerable way from the town that it was discovered that our Belgian ally was missing. One of our ambulances instantly turned back, after the two men in charge had transferred the wounded to another transport and had sent it on to the hospital. It must have required more than a little nerve to go back into Dixmude that night. The bombardment continued, and the two gentlemen were so long in returning that it was believed without doubt that some serious misadventure had overtaken them in their efforts to find the missing man. Without waiting very long, a second ambulance with two men went back into Dixmude to look for the first, and about midnight both of them returned, but, alas! without having been able to find our friend. It was a terribly anxious and trying time for every one, and the feelings of the little party can be imagined when they returned to Fumes without him. Every one remembered the fact that he had helped to load up the ambulances, and had called out "All right," but from that moment no tidings could be obtained of him, and there was no one to ask for information in the confused and tormented town.

However, all's well that ends well. When our spirits were at their lowest, he appeared at the door and explained that he had been obliged to descend into a cellar a second time to make sure that no wounded were left in it, and that when he came up into the air again there was no trace of the ambulances to be seen. He got out of the town on his feet, and was picked up later by a Belgian conveyance, which brought him to the door of the hospital.

Wherever our ambulances were wanted they always went, and I have never known a case of their turning back. Dixmude was a case in point, and there were many others which I could quote.

CHAPTER V.

ON my birthday [26 October]—one is a little apt to fix dates in this egotistic way in war time, because one's own personality is of so little account, and one is so small in the vastness of it that one clings to what there may be left of it as one recalls one's features in a mirror—I was out with the ambulances. I remember looking forward to my day in the open air very much, and feeling very saddened when I went over to the civil hospital with a wounded old woman, and found the nuns washing on the green there, and under a rude open shed I saw many dead laid. They were only partially covered with blankets, and I noticed how tired, even in death, their poor soiled feet looked. The nuns, with their black robes tucked up, went on with their washing, and the dead slept beside them.

It was very early, and dawn always suggests a forward look. One wanted something good for these unconsidered soldiers, with a number slung round their necks, who had given even their names for their country.

We started immediately after breakfast to go and bring in the wounded. It was a gusty, wild morning—one of those days when the sky takes up all the picture, and the world looks small. The mud was deep on either side of the cobbled roadway, and I heard the chauffeurs say that the ambulances steered badly, and that it was heavy going. When we reached the scene of action, it was necessary to put out of mind altogether the tin-soldier notion of battle, which one had learned upon the nursery floor. Squares and serried ranks and battalions are not visible—indeed, nothing was visible except the smoke of bursting shells. There was an air of untidiness, if one may so express it, which is very different from the straight lines of soldiers on the nursery carpet. First, one came to straggling lots of men covered with mud coming back from the trenches to rest, or a corps of bicyclists, perhaps, ploughing through the mud. Every one seemed bent on but two things—to lie down somewhere, and to get something to eat.

All the soldiers were squatting in groups behind the guns, trying to cook things. I saw one man with a couple of loaves spitted on his bayonet and carried over his shoulder, and another with half a sheep's carcass across his back. Still another—with a good deal of faith—was trying to tempt a fish out of the canal, with a line held on a piece of stick. After the straggling soldiers came a line of ammunition vans, and then the long gray guns, tilted at various angles, and beyond, the bursting shells like black and white tufts against the sky. The shells made noise enough; but the long gray guns, when we got beyond them, had a curious streaky sound.

I got an unexpected touch of humour when I saw one of our chauffeurs put out his hand to signal to a gun not to fire down our road, in exactly the manner of a "Bobby" regulating London traffic. And I was reminded of a funny sight I had seen in the city of Delhi, when one of the gorgeous elephants of the Durbar was swinging along in his lordly way in the middle of the road, and a small clerk in gray clothes and a topee, seated on a bicycle, came up behind and pinged his little bell to make the elephant move. These nationalized characteristics of English people endear them to one very much, even as one laughs at them.

When we came back to the road, which we had quitted for a time, we were directed where to find the wounded. By the roadside was a little house where, within, one could see surgeons in white coats busily dressing wounds, and some of these supplied cases for the stretcher-bearers, while others were to be found in the churches.

Nearly all the churches in Flanders were used for the soldiers, and their appearance was pitifully desolate. The chairs of the place were stacked together in the middle of the building, which was then filled with straw, and on this the men slept or rested, or ate their dinner, or nursed their wounds. Frequently there were great shell holes in the walls and roof. The altar always had the Host removed from it; but Calvaries still hung on the walls, and figures of saints with meek faces and sightless eyes, and virgins with gilt gowns, looked down on tired soldiers resting for a while before going out again to kill or to be killed.

One day, while the troops rested at Lamprinesse, a spy gave notice where they were, and probably directed the fire too, for the shells fell with horrible accuracy, killing and wounding on every side. I have often, indeed all the rime, at the station at Furnes, seen men coming in straight off the battlefield, but I have never seen any quite like those who came in that morning from the church at Lamprinesse. They were men who, no doubt, were accustomed to sleep heavily, and they had been rudely awakened. In their faces was a look of complete bewilderment, and they were dazed and unable to answer when one spoke to them, like dreamers who have seen some horrible vision.

The church which I saw first, with its straw-covered floor and the piled chairs and the deadly cold of it, remains in my mind as a scene of absolute desolation. Outside was a group of English men and women looking like a shooting party at home, but now engaged in finding out where wounded were, and bearing a hand with stretchers on which to take them away.

When we got back to the hospital there was an ambulance, as usual, in the yard, and I was surprised as we unbuttoned the canvas tilt to hear an English voice from inside. We had not before had English patients, as we were quite away from the British lines, and it was amazing to hear one's own tongue from a wounded man. The voice from within the ambulance went on, "Just give the poor chap above me a drop of water, will you? He is pretty bad."

We drew the curtain back, and discovered a man with a cigar in his mouth, laughing gaily.

"Best joke in the world," he said—"both my legs broken, and you'll have to lift me out. Give the chap above me some water first. I am all right."

The man was Mr. Reading—"Dick Reading," as I always heard him affectionately called. He was serving with the Belgian army, and, as we subsequently heard, he was standing behind a gun-carriage when a shell burst close to him, breaking both his legs. The gun-carriage started at a gallop, and Mr. Reading caught hold of it and held on behind, and was dragged in this fashion for some hundreds of yards, his legs being useless, but he himself conscious and determined to hold on and get away from bursting shells. He was taken to the operating theatre, and I did not see him again till the afternoon, when, having been under chloroform, he was concerned to know whether he had "behaved like a baby."

We wished we could have kept Mr. Reading with us, but every patient had to be cleared out of the hospital, as we were under orders to evacuate Furnes.

We went the next day to Poperinghe, thirty miles off, and although, as it turned out, the move was unnecessary and we came back again in two days, the drive there was extraordinarily interesting. On either side of the road troops from every part of the world seemed to be assembled. There were Arabs with flowing robes and fine clothes, and there were Turcos with baggy trousers, and English Tommies, and French Chasseurs. They were nearly all cooking things for supper, and the waning sunset and the ruddy light of the fires made the whole scene wonderfully picturesque.

We found beds ready for us in a convent at Poperinghe (and remarkably welcome they were), but there was nothing to eat, and we went and bought chops, which we cooked in a little cafe, which smelled of burned fat.

One was glad to renew one's acquaintance with the British soldiers, whom one met everywhere, and who were invariably cheerful and full of jokes. To the nurses who passed, they merely said, "No, miss, not yet!" and in rain or in sun their spirits never failed.

There was not much to do at Poperinghe, and we were glad to get back to Furnes, although our welcome there consisted of some shells, which fell close to the hospital, and were picked up by souvenir grafters. While there wasn't much to do, I made one of those excursions, which were afterwards so stringently forbidden, to Nieuport. One wishes one had had more of them. But I happened to be busy most of the time. Nieuport had been heavily shelled for some time by both German and Allies' guns, and in its wretched and ruined condition it seemed to me like some town that one sees in a nightmare. Some houses were still left standing when I was there, and have probably since disappeared; but there was not a pane of glass in the place, and few buildings that had not been touched.

41

Roofs were gone and frontages had fallen forward into the streets, leaving simple domestic interiors exposed. The brutality of the whole thing struck one painfully, and the expo-sure of humble dwellings and the naked desolation of it all were piteous in their simple tragedy.

There was something about Nieuport which seemed to me like the people who had fought for it—something kindly and domestic and given to inexpensive little pleasures, and now most cruelly wronged and yet uncomplaining. The shattered walls and wrecked windows and the fallen front-ages at Nieuport gave me many a glimpse into little insignificant houses, with supper set on the kitchen table, and little ornaments still left stand-ing on the chimney-piece above the stove. Here, where the outer wall was gone, one saw a whole section of a house, as when one opens the front of a doll's house and sees the upper and the lower stories displayed. The servants' rooms in the upper attics, with their tin boxes and pendent dresses, had descended to the basement, and a baby's cradle hung between the floors. The iron of the bedsteads was twisted into strange shapes, and pictures waved despondently on the walls. In the roadway outside were great holes where shells had fallen, and at an inlaid table of great beauty that stood in the garden, some soldiers ate their breakfast and cut their bread with their clasp knives. Many of the houses were completely hollowed out by fire, but there was one toy shop at a corner where a counter and shelves remained, although doors and windows were gone. The little shop was filled with the dust and debris of fallen roof and wrecked windows; there were holes made by shells, and the inner walls lay in one helpless mass on the floor, while the upper part of the house was wrecked.

Across the ceiling a line of elastic hung and remained, where solid things had all been destroyed and had fallen, and on the elastic line was a row of bobbing, foolishly grinning dolls, with eyes that still gleamed behind the dust that covered them, and painted lips that smirked. When the wind blew through the empty casement the dolls all danced upon their rubber line, and in the curious quiet of the deserted town their waxen feet beating together made a little pattering sound.

The cathedral was roofless, but had an outer wall and two half-ruined aisles standing when I was in Nieuport, the trees all round it were slashed and scorched by shell-fire, and the autumn leaves which still hung on them were burnt up and shrivelled. In a furniture-shop, goods were exposed for sale, and some advertisements had a futile look about them like trivial things viewed from some large eternity.

Death was almost consciously present in this little town where so many have fallen, and the poor small houses in the humbler streets seemed to hold out piteous protesting hands to one, as though, like other non-combatants in this hideous war, they were asking why they had sustained these terrible hurts.

The following Sunday there was an important meeting at Dunkirk of Lord Kitchener [Field Marshal Horatio Herbert Kitchener, 1st Earl Kitchener], Mr. [Winston] Churchill, General French, General Joffre, and Monsieur Poincare. I was on my way to Calais to meet some ladies who were returning from England, and had the pleasure of seeing some of these celebrated men. The ladies did not arrive, and I stayed for a time at Dunkirk and gave what help I could at the station there. The great railway shed was known by the ghastly name of "The Shambles," and it merited the sobriquet. On the first occasion that I visited it, it was in the company of a naval doctor, who had gone there with the intention of dressing some of the untended wounds. But so bad was the atmosphere of the place that he declared it was impossible to remove a single bandage.

A long platform ran down the middle of the shed, and the railway lines on either side of it were covered with straw. On these the wounded and sick lay in numbers so large that I fear to give them without corroboration from others who worked there. Two ladies gave the numbers as something exceeding a thousand a night. The men had been brought by train from every part of the country to be put on hospital ships or to go to England, and they waited transportation in the sheds, lying on the golden straw in their dark uniforms, and looking, it seemed to me, like nothing so much as shot pheasants laid out in rows after some big shoot in the coverts. The lights burned very dimly in the huge place, because lights always must burn dimly in war time, and there were no stoves. It was winter weather, and from the train half-frozen men used to pour into the sheds in their torn uniforms, whose seams had been for the most part slit up to give place to bandages. It touched one inexpressibly to see each one's care of his wound, for one felt that, however difficult realization might be of suffering on so large a scale, every man in this most pitiful band was bearing pain and bearing it alone. As they alighted from the train or passed through the doorway of the shed, their poor hands used to be put out to prevent an accidental touch from anything, and all that seemed to keep them alert in the comfortless cold was the fear of being hurt afresh.

No one ever complained. It was *la guerre*. Upon this scene of desolation—and I have feared to picture it too vividly—came some ladies, so vigorous and at the same time so careful, that much was accomplished by them in a very short space of time. The odious and heavy smell of the great sheds gave place to sanitation, and a lean-to kitchen was put up at small cost, where soup and coffee were made. Dressing-stations were established at either end of the sheds, where surgeons and nurses worked all day and all night. Wounded Germans got attention with the rest, and stoves were distributed all down the sheds, while on the long platform, clean straw mattresses were laid out in rows, and a band of workers came each night to give soup and to attend to the sick.

There was one aspect of work in the war which struck me so often that it seems worth while mentioning it here. There were difficulties—there were bound to be difficulties at first—and with the enormous number of men pouring through the country, the dislocation to traffic was often unavoidable, just as it was impossible to raise hospitals all over the country in a night. One's astonishment was that things arranged themselves so quickly! One's astonishment increased when one found that hardly a thing which the soldier has wanted in this war has been denied him. Money has poured in from all sides. There has scarcely been, even in those journals which are famous for exploiting grievances, a single genuine case of unrelieved distress or of suffering made worse by want of care or forethought. It seems to me that never have sacrifices been made more willingly and never have men and women worked with more disinterested and splendid endeavour than during this war.

The aspect of it which I have to consider is that in many cases—as in the matter of the station at Dunkirk, for instance—an evil which had existed and had remained unremedied for a considerable time, was discovered and overcome by the tireless work of a few individuals. It was in affairs of this sort that women excelled. They seem to have an eye for detail and a capacity for treating even large numbers individually which is admirable and I believe uniquely feminine. Their vigour and their non-acceptance of impossibilities are factors also in the success of their undertakings.

The thing that strikes one unfavourably sometimes is that, when work has been established, order restored, and that "first step," which costs so much, has been made, the Voice of Authority (one is obliged to write the words with initials) can be heard making rules, dismissing workers, and abrogating to itself full command of the work which has been so hardly wrought. Even where its influence is not so drastic as this it issues rules and regulations and frames notices hung on nails. The initiative which has had the courage to launch schemes becomes hidebound and even penalized. And workers, turned away from the doors of their own workshops or regulated by a ticket of entrance, are relegated to that humble corner which is known as "their proper place."

One hardly ventures to specialize instances of this sort which might only provoke discussion, and would, as our leading politician always says, "serve no useful purpose." But they occurred often enough to induce the belief that in the aggregate they might furnish food for thought.

It was still possible to get permits and passports to Dunkirk up till the month of November, and one met many friends unexpectedly arrived from England and elsewhere. A large number of hospitals was being installed, and money seemed to be forthcoming for everything.

It has been my lot to see a little of warfare before this present crisis. I happened to be present at the bombardment of Rio de

Janeiro, and later, I and some friends rode through the Balkans—not during the actual war, but when much fighting and still more massacring were going on. I was fortunate enough to find work to do in the South African War, and I believe I may call this present war my fourth campaign. And after such experience as I have had (and much more that I have read about) I should be inclined to say that in the matter of care of the sick and wounded, and abundance of food and clothing, there has never been a war which has left one so little to regret, and almost the only thing forgotten seems to have been ammunition. The number of workers has been large and efficient, the organization has been good, and where mistakes have been made or grievances discovered, they have been put right as soon as possible. At first, every one suffered from the unpreparedness which distinguished the outset of the struggle, but I think there has been nothing that has wrung one's heart as in the awful tales of the wounded in the Crimea, nor has there been unnecessary suffering for any great length of time. This, I believe, must be consoling to all those who at home are grieving over the necessary horrors which war brings.

In the matter of transport alone, the difference between fighting in South Africa and fighting four hours from London can hardly be exaggerated. A man wounded to-day in Flanders sits up in his cot at Netley for his breakfast to-morrow, and rubber-tyred ambulances convey their burdens swiftly, and as much as possible painlessly, to field hospitals or to the base. As soon as a man is found he can be sure of attention. The tragedy of suffering hangs round those who are not found or who remain undiscovered for days, and of this one had many and most painful instances at Fumes station. Still, one was able to feel thankful for the difference between motor ambulances and Kafir ox wagons, with their grievous jolting journeys of perhaps seven days before a hospital was reached, or the long, slow-moving trains where one used to see English soldiers lying on the floors or under the seats with their boots for pillows!

If war has grown more hideous—as of course it has done, and it is daily becoming worse—it has at the same time become more merciful; and during the long pause in the winter's fighting, time

46

and opportunity were found for arranging and preparing comforts on a generous scale.

At first, as I have said, nothing was in order. Our field hospital was sending off cases every day which ought never to have left the wards had space been available; and they were sending them off, too, in trucks lined with straw and with neither lights nor attendants nor the means of getting the men so much as a cup of water.

I believed that a soup kitchen might be useful at Fumes station, and I, with three Belgian Sisters, established one there.

CHAPTER VI.

WHILE the kitchen was being installed at Furnes a message reached me that one of my nephews had been wounded at Ypres, and I was fortunate enough to get a car returning to Boulogne, in which I was able to go to him at once.

This first Battle of Ypres [October 19–November 22, 1914; estimates of casualties on all sides varies but were in the multiple tens of thousands] has not, I believe, been fully, or at least, generally understood yet. One does not like to deal in superlatives, but it is hardly too much to say that it was one of the great events of our history, and probably there are not many battles that can compare with it. A sergeant returning wounded said to me, "It was proper 'ell, miss." The battle had, indeed, something about it which suggests things so infernal that the sergeant's remark alone seems to describe it. The weather was thick and heavy during the prolonged fighting in and around the old town, and in the stillness one could hear the guns very far away. The air was dour with smoke, and news was pitifully scarce. Men were dying in numbers too large for us to dare to count, and one never heard who had fallen or who was safe.

Only in years to come shall we hear all about it. Soldiers themselves will always probably say very little. Hardly anyone ever talks about hell when they have been there! It is only by a chance word or a chance conversation here and there that one will learn much.

Here and now, it seems hardly a digression to speak of the work done by what are called "The Regulars" in war time. As I have belonged to two voluntary corps, I am, perhaps, one of o¹ those persons who are privileged to say something on the matter. For I feel that voluntary work has had its well-deserved meed of praise, and that its really splendid work has been handsomely acknowledged. The real business of war is, however, in the hands of the regular army, the Territorials, the Colonial troops, and other trained military bodies, and the nursing is done by regular certificated women. These and the soldiers are not often photographed, except in those blurred and indistinct groups that

48

one sees in the morning papers, and they seldom have the chance of appearing individually before the eyes of the world. At Ypres one learned what plain unsung British line regiments can do; while it is noted of one regiment of Guards that they have never given up a trench! Plain soldiers, doing their duty plainly and unpretentiously, under circumstances which cannot fitly be described either by the familiar term of "frightfulness" or "horror," won the Battle of Ypres.

Some generals know this. There was a moment when regiments were falling back, and two men watching the battle may have despaired or they may not. At any rate, other men say their faces were white and the order was given to retire, when one of them exclaimed, "My God, the—s are sticking it!"....

They say the general tried three times to thank the regiment who had saved the day, and was unable to do so.

Every man knew that success or failure lay with himself! Their manner of meeting death was always heroic, and worthy of the names which they bore. The list of names is a good one and highly esteemed amongst us. In the roll of honour one is reminded of a calling-over at Eton, where so many names have an historical interest! One need not particularize them; all the best of English birth and of English manhood were there. The men whose forefathers fought at Agincourt, or Crecy, or Waterloo, carried the old names unstained at the Battle of Ypres.

It is the name that counts; and one might write a volume on the subject! It is the name that is the real meaning of a "scrap of paper," and the honour of a thing lies in the fact that when a man has put his signature to it he sticks by it. There were men at Ypres who died for the sake of a tradition, or for the sake of the names of their regiments.

We are only getting news of it all now, in the tales that boys tell in hospital, or that soldiers write home from the front; and we are getting the tales told jerkily and inconsequently, as I got them in the hospital at Boulogne. No one was up to very much talking, and at one bed one heard only of a man's wounds, while at another, bits of news came unexpectedly, or a chance word would conjure up a

49

recollection of the fight. One learned then what, perhaps, we 'had hardly realized before, that the British cheerfulness and the amazingly good jokes which they make are not confined to the pauses of battle, but are shouted out from the very lines of firing, and are irrepressible even in the trenches.

"Don't get downhearted, my dear!" Thomas Atkins calls out to his German foe only thirty yards away from him. "You have started for home, and you will soon be travelling a little faster than you want to!"

"I'm only firing in order to give my lady-friends flower vases," says an impertinent boy behind a gun, knowing how fond women are of brass shell-cases. And two Irishmen settle a long-standing quarrel between them by having it out with fists under heavy shellfire.

Here is a "home-like" description of a trench:—

"*April* 23rd, 1915.

"The trenches here are only about seventy yards apart, and ours are very good in places, while one part, called the Keep, has been made into a sort of rock-garden with various battalions' badges worked in shrubs, and a certain number of flowers planted. The paths between are bricked with the remains of walls, etc.—all very clean. It apparently was the courtyard of a farm at one time."

A boy friend scribbles for me the type of letter a soldier writes— what he says in it, what he says afterwards:—

Before:

"Dear mum, dad, wife, and child,—I now take great pleasure in writing you these few lines, hoping they will find you in good health, as it leaves me at present. We have had a lot of fighting lately, and have had a good few casualties. Poor old Bill has gone, and Alf is wounded. I thank God, He has preserved me so far. Give my regards to Nell, and tell her I would give a lot to be with her now. I hope Lizzie is getting the money all right. She ought to write about it if she ain't. Well, God bless you all. From your dear boy, BERT."

Afterwards:

"Damn, boy, come on now; there's three mucking in that tin of jam. Garn, boy, I tell you it is so. Ask the sergeant! There! You! Didn't I well say so? An' I don't want no -- old buck, or I'll knock your -- face in! "

The same boy writes:

"Scene: A trench. Time: One hour before dawn. Silence only broken by stentorian snores (no one in the world snores like the British soldier). One receives a dig in the ribs like the kick of a horse, and hears a gruff voice:

Sir! Sir! Beg pardon, sir; four o'clock, sir.'

"One opens one's eyes and recognizes the burly sergeant of the guard. With an oath one tells him to wake the men and tell them to get to their fire positions, and one gets up oneself from one's covering of straw or overcoat. The injunction to 'Stand to arms!' and hardly suppressed langwidge announce to one that the company is waking up. The voice of the company wit can be distinguished:

"Good morning, gentlemen. And how am I? Sausages, eggs and bacon, kippahs, ham, tea or coffeeh. What! only bully and biscuit? Nevah mind; very nourishing.'

"Wit hastily suppressed under the livery eye of the company captain:

"Not so much talking there. Put out that cigarette. Do you want to get a bullet in the mouth, fool! Pass the word. No smoking before dawn. Quartermaster-sergeant!' (Arrival of same.)

"Sir!"

"Is there any tea for the men this morning?"

"No, sir; company cooker couldn't come up, sir, on account of shell-fire." (Much stamping of feet and audible curses.)

"Quartermaster-sergeant: There's a hissue of rum, sir. Shall I give it out, sir?"

"No. Wait till daylight."

"Very good, sir."

"In this manner one gets through the horrible hour of standing to arms before dawn.

"We were marching back for a short rest after rather a hot engagement," the boy says. "One of our men remarked in a jocose manner, Are we downhearted? ' Instead of the usual chorus of 'No,' a little man near me said quietly, 'Let every one speak for himself.'

"Having lunched one morning on the Aisne, a sergeant said in broad Scotch, Aye, I think I got some o' them the morn! They put their heids a wee thing too high aboon the bracken! However, I'm awa' noo to mak' sure.' He came back and said, Aye, they're lying oot as dead's mutton! He was a born sniper, and revelled in it. If there was nothing doing with his own regiment, he would join another for the' sake of killing a German. And he continuedi cdaein' his wee bit,' as he called it, until he himself was killed."

I heard from another soldier that during a charge he passed a Highlander who appeared to be badly wounded, and he thought he was dead; but on returning he found him sitting up humming a Scottish ballad, and picking his tartan hose out of a wound in his leg with his bayonet.

When soldiers win the V.C. [Victoria Cross] they ask, "What for?" and are as surprised as when they have won a "Tit-Bits" competition. "I didn't do much," they say; "there was a poor chap outside and I brought him in." They laugh at everything except the death of their comrades, and what they do not laugh at they grumble at; and above all, they must have nicknames for everything. And "Jack Johnsons," and "Beer barrels," and "Mothers," and "Black Marias" have an absurd sound about them which must be maddening for Germans. A nation which preaches a gospel of hate would doubtless like something more serious in return for what it feels! But Englishmen do not feel hate, although they very often feel rage. And now even Germans are trying to write little comic letters which they drop from Taubes, but none of them are very witty.

Side by side with the Britishers' little jokes death stalks grimly. One regiment went into the campaign 1,100 strong, and now only 73 are left. Another counted its numbers by 1,350 men: they had not quite 300 left after the Battle of Ypres. One knows of another regiment who were in the trenches for three weeks, and buried their dead there, and lived on amongst the straw and muck. One hears a boy cry out " Stick it, the "Welch! " with his last breath, just as he used to call it out at football matches and, the like, and of another who had only breath enough left to whisper, " Have we won? " A middy of fifteen on board ship, suspecting uneasiness on the part of his men under heavy fire, gathers a group of them round him, and sitting down he gravely consults with them as to whether they consider that the new engineer is shaping well.

When they lie ill in bed we try to keep from them the newspapers which tell of the colonel fallen or the comrade gone. For our own part we believe that we shall not very easily find the like of these good men again. There is on especially whom we recall. He was a very chivalrous person, and a most courteous an charming friend. It seems to us as though, when Colonel—died something fine and good died with him. We remember his loyalty to his friends, and the courage which faced with every day, health that was far from good. We heard of him that the wound he had received would not, perhaps, have killed a man of more robust physique, but that he had had no sleep for four nights, and that while the bullet had done little more than graze him, he was utterly tired and slept, and so continues to sleep.

There are those who envy him even now. There are old comrades of his who watched the regiment march away, who have only one feeling of regret, and that is that they were not with him.

Days in hospital are very long, and for some men the memory of what they have seen has gone very deep, and they try to tell one what it is like to be eight or fourteen days under shell-fire, but they are unable to do so, and stop and say, "It was beastly!"

A boy with a little table beside him covered with things which he cannot eat, and a packet of "goodies," which shows how young he is, rolls round in his bed, and says it is "beastly" for the other fellows to hear him groaning when he is not quite himself o' nights. His companion says, "You see, what is pretty ghastly is that when you have taken a trench or lost one, the wounded are often left out in the open. You can't reach them" (the boy turns in bed again and puts his arms out on the sheets). "It is impossible to get at them," he says; "sometimes they die of starvation within sight of us. We see them raise themselves on an arm for a minute, and yell to us to come to them, but we can't. Yes, at Ypres the Germans got our range to an inch, and began shelling our trenches. A whole company next me was wiped out. It was beastly! "

One boy has to take a message to his colonel, and the communication trench by which he goes is not quite finished. So the boy climbs out into the open, and races across to where the unfinished trench begins again. He is not aware, of course, that a boy running for his life should strike one in a pathetic light!

He was badly hit, but he managed just to tumble into the next bit of trench, where two men found him. He was bound up and carried four miles on crossed rifles to the hospital at Ypres, and then the train journey had to begin. Fortunately, morphia does its work.

"I got half my men away," says an infant, with his moustache not grown, "but I lost the rest." And when he is asked how he spent his nineteenth birthday in the trenches, he replies in a voice hardly audible through weakness, "got up early and killed a German!"

When they are better the last thing they ever want to talk about is the bad times they have had; and, quite wholesomely, they have an in-satiable desire for picture papers and *revues*. It is a good thing to be alive after all!

Our King's visit [George V] to Flanders did every one good. There was a review held in the Grand Place at Furnes, and the Belgian soldiers, who are enthusiasts, turned out well. There were some pretty black days just then, when the water lay all round the little town where we lived and the nights were cold and wet. Oddly enough, war has a dull side to it, as soldiers know. But there was a good time coming, and even although the print at the top of newspaper sheets was not always very large, we were holding on, and that was everything. The King knew this; and we knew that he knew it.

54

CHAPTER VII.

FURNES.

THE first soup kitchen was a very small, dark little place. It was really only a small space under an archway, and cut off from the rest of the station by a door of sacking stretched on a wooden frame. The actual space within the room measured eight feet by seven feet, and in this not very lordly apartment was a small stove which burned, and a large one which didn't. There were a few kettles and pots, and a little coffee grinder, too, with a picture of a blue windmill on it, for which I conceived an earnest hatred, such as inanimate things sometimes inspire in one! It was so silly and so in- adequate, and in order to get enough ground coffee its futile little handle had to be turned all day, while the blue windmill looked busy and did nothing, and was perfectly cheerful all the time.

With these not very useful tools to work with (and it was very difficult to buy anything at Furnes at that time), there came a rush of work, which is not unusual in war time, and there was a great deal to do at the kitchen.

The first convoy of wounded men used to come in about 10.30 a m. They arrived always in one of those road trains which are common in Belgium, and which make circuits and stop at various small stations. We used to hear a horn blown, and then the noisy outer door of the station slammed, and we knew the train-load of men had arrived. The "sitting cases" were always brought in first. These were men damaged for the most part in their feet or hands, or with superficial scalp wounds, or frost bitten. They hobbled in, or were carried on men's backs, or leaned against some comrade's shoulder. And across the entrance hall of the station went, day and night, a long stream of them, to pass under the archway, and out at the other side of the hall, and so on to the waiting train on the platform. It was a little pathetic to find how many soldiers thought they would have to pay for what was served to them, and to find them diving into their poor pockets for coins! They used to refuse cigarettes until quite sure that they were a free-will offering.

The *brancard* (stretcher) cases arrived next. They were all men who were *gravement blesses—one* learned the term too well!—and they were laid in rows on the floor of the entrance hall of the station. All were quite helpless!—wounded men with a number round their necks and a label on their coats, pinned there by the surgeon at the first dressing-station! I never saw any one of them look about him or take the smallest interest in his surroundings. They had been sent into the trenches, and had had a bullet through them, or a piece of shell, and they had been put into ambulances and labelled and sent somewhere. I think many of them were quite unaware that they were in a station. A steaming basin of coffee or soup revived them greatly, and even having to decide which of these refreshments they would have, and helping themselves to bread, pulled them together a little. Otherwise they most often seemed dazed and with no thought for anything but their wounds. One was struck by their silence. No one spoke or even, except on rare occasions, moaned much. There was that dogged patient Flemish tenacity about them which seldom expresses itself in words. They were soldiers dumbly enduring, and the sight impressed me afresh every day.

There was just one thing which added a good deal (and unnecessarily, I think) to the suffering of the wounded men, and it might be avoided, I believe. It was the difference in the size of the stretchers used for transportation. The patterns were different and the sizes were different. Now stretchers, both in ambulances and in trains, have to be slung, and must fit into the sockets provided for them. So that it is obvious that a uniform size should be maim tamed. But the ambulance stretchers are ark inch and a half too wide for the train; and the Belgian, French, and English patterns all differ slightly from each other. (The Belgian one seemed to me to be the best, while the French had the best ambulances.) The consequence of this was that the wounded men were constantly being shifted from one stretcher to another. The men on the ambulances, or on the road train which brought them in, were unable to carry them directly to the train and sling them into the sockets which were fixed there. But each stretcher had to be placed upon the floor, and then the unhappy man who lay on it was lifted on to a train-stretcher laid alongside of it. If his uniform was fairly

56

sound, or he was a Turco with baggy trousers, the *brancardiers* could take hold of these and make them serve as a sort of sling to transfer the patient. But many of the men who came in were in rags, or their clothes had been cut by the surgeon, and the process of shifting them was horribly painful, and frequently produced cries which they were unable to stifle. When they reached their destination at the base the same shifting process had to be gone through. Added to this, there was always an outcry about lost stretchers and complaints about the different patterns getting mixed.

If it is too late now, or too expensive, to provide stretchers of the same pattern for three armies, I do not think it would be at all difficult to make the sockets in the ambulances expanding rather than fixed, or there might be an alternative socket on which the larger stretchers might be placed.

It used to make one miserable that, for the sake of one and a half inches of space, men should be put to such real agony as transferring them frequently involved. I asked a surgeon who came to visit the station to write to the Press about this, for I felt sure that a word from him would mean much more than many words from me. But I could never hear of anything being done.

When the men were in the train we used to take them hot coffee and soup and bread. I had a little red hand-cart which was very useful in this respect, and which, for some unknown reason, always delighted the soldiers. And afterwards, through the kindness of the people of the parish of Coldstream in Scotland, two very superior soup carriages were sent to me, with trays for bread, and a fire to keep the soup hot.

Lately, since the warmer weather has come, in, and since new regulations have been made about feeding the wounded in the hall of Adenkerke station—and not in the train—these carriages have been presented to the Belgian army, who are delighted with them.

There was a good deal of desultory shelling going on at Furnes in those days, although no actual bombardment. One morning, when I was giving out my soup at the train and the Belgian Sisters their coffee, three shells came with their unpleasant scream into the station. The first passed disagreeably close just overhead. Afterwards, in order to enhance my value in the eyes of my relatives and friends, I persuaded a friend of mine to take a photograph of the big hole which it made in a wall that was just behind me. Beyond the wall was a huge hay store, and in the closely packed bales of hay the shell, no doubt, ended itself. But we picked up pieces of it quite hot, and, alas! the flying fragments killed two men in the station, while another man showed me his watch crumpled up like a piece of paper by a bit of shell.

Every window and every breakable thing in the train was shattered by the impact of the explosion, and it was a bad moment for helpless men lying within, and unable to stir or help themselves. The train was stationary, and had no engine attached to it, and had the shelling continued, it might have been very serious for them. But there was no more of it that day.

At Cuxide, however, there had been a considerable bombardment, and the refugees were flying into Furnes, and were being evacuated by our ambulances. All of them were destitute, having been obliged to leave everything behind them, and their large numbers made feeding them a little difficult. However, we did what we could, and I was rather pleased with the exploits of the kitchen that day. Its actual output of liquid always seemed, I thought, to be in excess of its size; but on that day we had been asked unexpectedly to give breakfast to 260 men going into the trenches, and after-wards there were about 80 or 100 refugees to feed twice, besides all the wounded, who some-times now numbered about so per day.

Sometimes a soldier would come in and help in the kitchen, and my own friends were most kind in looking in at night when I was alone, and not only helped to take soup to the train, but often assisted me to cut up vegetables; and would frequently keep me company before the last convoy came in, which was generally between eleven o'clock and midnight. The three Belgian Sisters took entire charge of preparing the coffee and worked from early morning till 6 p m., and we had a better coffee grinder now. I was told to keep the little blue windmill one in case it should come in useful. But I gave it to a soldier when no one was looking, and was glad to get rid of it!

The work divided itself into shifts, which made it easier than might be imagined. The convoys came in at 10.30, at 4 o'clock (at which time some of the Fumes ladies helped to pass food round), and again at near midnight. The midnight convoy always seemed to me the most sad, as it certainly often was the largest that arrived. The men used to come in half-frozen from the road-train (which there was no means of warming), and were hardly able to walk. Very many of them had frost-bitten feet through standing in the bitter cold water knee-deep in the trenches. Every one wore bandages which gleamed white in the light of the dim oil lamp that burned in the big entrance hall of the station, and I used sometimes to think that only the pen of a Zola could fittingly describe the scene.

When it was possible, I used to place my soup-cart under the lamp, and ladle out the soup as the men entered. But this plan had to be given up later because of the number of stretcher-cases that came in and had to be laid on the floor.

The order used to be given out, "Preparez vos quarts, s'il vous plait, Messieurs," and the men would search stiffly in their wallets for the little tin cups they carried with them. Under the smoky lamp one saw one's *marmite* filled with its steaming mixture, and above it hands of every colour—brown, white, or black—holding out their tin cups. There were dim forms beyond, and frosty breaths, and bandages showing white in the gloom, and one heard rather than saw the men drinking soup. Then they passed out under the archway, and one somewhat prosaically cleaned up the kitchen and walked home through the dark little town with one's lantern gleaming on seas of mud!

Very naturally there was a considerable number of strangers who looked in to see what was going on at the kitchen, and these also were so kind as to lend a hand sometimes with distributing soup. One began to separate the sheep from the goats, and to classify one's visitors!

There was one particular class whom I always called "This-poor-fellow-has-had-none." I saw these both at the station and in hospitals. Their attitude (which, I am sure, was quite unconscious) always seemed to be that until they arrived on the scene—and they seldom stayed long!—no one had had any proper attention.

In the wards one used to see them stop some busy nurse to say, "The man in the corner must have some water;" he says (reproachfully) "he has asked for it three times." That the man had been forbidden water never seemed to occur to them. Their intentions were good, but they were not always very useful. Their graceful attitude as they stooped over a sick man was often connected with requiring many things passed to them, and they were really not so much help as, I am sure, they meant to be. I was always glad when "This-poor-fellow-has-had-none" departed, for the indiscriminate feeding of sick men is attended with a certain amount of danger.

There were many other types for whom one often tried to find an adjective. In particular were those persons who, whenever there was news of a reverse, always said, "Why don't we *do* something?" and others who meant "to get things straightened out," and there were two types who were the antithesis of each other, one whom I called " I-won't-be-bossed," and the other " I-will-be-crowned." But all of them had excellent points, and the average of humanity was, as usual, good. They took the rough with the smooth, and even enjoyed the rough, or denied that it existed. I heard an apology made to a delightful visitor, who came to see us at Fumes for two days, and to whom a not very appetizing breakfast was offered. She replied in her cordial way, "I have done very well, indeed, thank you. I have had a nice piece of bread and some excellent margarine."

As a matter of fact, that margarine was not excellent. It was proved afterwards to be some that had been discarded by the Royal Navy as unfit for consumption; its odour was certainly strong, and I had had grave suspicions about it from the first.

Some "good sorts" who were bent on roughing it, seemed to believe that war and a want of house linen were inseparable, while a scarcity of hand-towels was obligatory! In this matter, abstention

60

was easy, for I never remember an overabundance of them. But then, one must admit that the supply was somewhat depleted by the uses they were put to, and I have seen them serving as pillow-slips, dinner-napkins, tablecloths, pocket-handkerchiefs, and for Jane to sleep on

Jane was a dog. She was large and red, and with a boisterous manner, and she had been found by one of our party at Pervyse, and given a home at Furnes. As a refugee one was obliged to give Jane a welcome; but as a dog she was not a success. She never took things seriously, and she always pretended to be asleep when she had taken the best place (on which she always left a legacy of red hair). But she had a gift of cadging for meals which almost raised her to distinction. I have seen her myself looking longingly at food at the villa until some was placed on the floor beside her; and later—for she really was not a dog of high character—she had exactly the same wistful appeal in her eye at the hospital, until some one said, "The poor brute is starving;" while a visit to the butcher's shop would disclose the fact that some charitable Belgians were feeding her under the table. I never heard if anyone murdered Jane later on (she developed a habit of appropriating gloves and candles); but I fancy she was given to some unfortunate Belgian officer, who may even have had to look pleased with the gift. She disappeared out of our lives, and only the red hair, which somehow she managed to knit skilfully into every cushion she sat on, remains as a memorial of her.

The butcher's shop was a feature in our variable *ménage* for a time. There was a sort of restaurant beyond it, where we had our meals. At night as one came back through the butcher's shop, one used to find oneself running into sheep's carcasses, for everything was very dark in Furnes. One carried a lantern everywhere, and sometimes it showed strange unexpected "war pictures"—a regiment sleeping under an archway, and once, in the covered way through which I had to pass, a whole batch of troop horses, tightly packed, under whose heads and tails I had to dodge to reach my door! And above all things, and through and over all things, it showed one mud!

There may have been something providential in the fact that rain fell so constantly and so heavily as it did in Flanders last winter—shut-ting out, as floods do, the foe; and one can only say that, under other circumstances, one could have done with a little less of it.

Christmas Day was brighter and very cold. I believe that in many parts of the fighting-line a truce was held, and soldiers forgathered, and firing ceased for a time. At Furnes it began before dawn, and I heard the cannon as I walked home about r a m.

At 6 o'clock High Mass was celebrated in the largest ward in the hospital; a temporary altar had been erected by the priests amidst the gay decorations with which the nurses and doctors had brightened the bare walls. The altar candles made little points of flame in the big darkness of the place, and a boy's voice filled the ward with his exquisite singing. Everywhere, across the room and round the windows, were the bright wreaths and paper decorations of Christmas, and beyond the Christmas trees, with their little presents dancing on the boughs, was the high altar at the far end of the room. It was a curious scene, half-pagan, half-Christian. Dimly, and almost like a personal memory, came the thought of an ancient worship—of a people who walked in darkness, no doubt, and yet who made sacred all that they knew of the best, and who did reverence to the berried plant, whose roots touched not earth, but grew between it and heaven, and who heard what the wind was saying, and knew trees to be their brothers and their gods. While the forward memory, catching a radiance from the palely burning candles on the altar, leapt to a diviner homage, and caught a fleeting vision of a greater light.

And all round the room wounded men lay in their narrow beds, and louder than the boy's voice at the Mass was the heavy sound of firing in the dim twilight of the morning.

Our own services were held in one of the schoolrooms, and there was some singing of Christmas hymns. At the station all was much as usual; but a wounded soldier, who had passed through there, sent a telegram to the *Ecossaise a la gare* wishing me a happy Christmas, and I was much touched by this.

In the afternoon there was an entertainment for all the refugee children at the civil hospital.

Two French officers once opened the door of the soup kitchen, and one said, "English, of course! No one else ever does anything for anybody."

I was reminded of the remark (which pleased me more than I like to say) when I was at the civil hospital on Christmas afternoon. When all our faults are made into a big heap and laid upon the scale, I do believe a few humble folk whom no one has ever heard about, will place on the other side of the balance a measure of English kindness. Very humbly I submit that this is a fine trait in a ruling race.

I wish I dared at this moment—and while the children are waiting for their Christmas tree—inflict my own views on some of the characteristics which have made us beloved and hated in the world. I wish I could think that anyone would be sufficiently interested to read a few remarks from me about the excellent hearts which blundering manners do their best to conceal, and the swagger which often covers a certain innate humility of which few people suspect our good Britisher. (I wonder if we should be at war with Germany now, did she not think we "tried to boss!")But, above all, there is that plain and unpretentious kindness which when it pities always puts its big rough hand into its pocket and says nothing about it. And I am not writing quite without knowledge of British kindness.

The piles of woollen goods alone which have passed through my own hands, and which I have seen pass through the hands of others during the war, have brought a message from home with them which has often moved me to tears. (On Christmas morning may one admit this!) The endless lines of khaki stitches which I have seen! the countless bales of socks and shirts and scarves which I have counted! and none of them—I can honestly say—have ever seemed to me mere scarves and socks and shirts, any more than wounded men seem to me to be "cases." Each one is stamped with a certain individuality and bears the touch of the maker's hand upon it, whether it be a wounded man or a pair of socks! and each one makes an appeal of its own. There are the socks with not quite enough of the same coloured wool to finish them, and the socks with the bit of extra wool to mend them, and the socks which have a tiny little present thrust inside them—a packet of chocolate or half a dozen cigarettes—and which give such an amazing amount of pleasure! An unknown friend in Scotland used to send small books of the Gospel of St. John in French in the toes of her socks—and very much were they liked. "Every-man"in Edinburgh sent me five boxes of groceries; and I had gifts from Benger's Food Company and the Tiptree Jam Works. To give away these things was always as great pleasure to me as it was to the men to receive them.

The scarves and socks and vests meant the work of people at home! These workers never had the stimulus of seeing for themselves the needs of the men, nor did they have the pleasure of bestowing their own gifts. Yet the supply never ceased, and the quality was always of the best. They represented hours of toil—and the wool was not got for nothing!

On this very Christmas afternoon, I remember working in the storeroom with a friend of mine, and we were discussing the boxes of tobacco which had been received, and the sacks of knitted things which came so easily that perhaps it was excusable sometimes to forget that they did not drop from heaven like dew! My friend drew from a very small parcel a little note which said: "We should like to send more, but money is very scarce this week."

Is it any wonder that one didn't see socks and scarves and Balaclava helmets quite clearly for a minute or two!...

The children's Christmas Tree was a great success, and they sang "God sef our nobbler king" (in English), and nearly lost their heads, poor babies, over simple boxes of English toys. They had lost much since the 1st of August, but they and their English allies have found each other in a very remarkable way. And if anyone wants joy over presents, he can come to Belgian children for it!

Many of the little creatures were wounded, and in the hospital was a dear little boy who was always called the Civilian. One mite was introduced to me as "Une blessee, Madame," and the women had the clothes they stood up in and nothing else in the world. But they all enjoyed Christmas Day, I think, and we came away after the treat with that parishy feeling which so intimately recalls England, and is generally connected with "taking a little rest now that it is all over."

While taking the required rest in a remarkably cold room, we were disturbed by shells, one of which came with its usual unexpectedness and its long whistling shriek quite close to the hospital. (Somehow one never expects a shell!) The next minute a child was brought in covered with dust and dirt, and crying bitterly. Her mother had been badly wounded and her arm completely blown off before the child's eyes.

She got immediate attention, of course. But the shelling did not cease till about 8.15, when we had a very cheery Christmas dinner, with crackers and speeches, and turkey, and plum-pudding. In all the wards and the refectories, etc., the fare was the same as our own. But few Belgians could "stick" the plum-pudding, and, indeed, one wondered whether a Christmas pudding or Christmas shells require the greater amount of nerve.

CHAPTER VIII.

FURNES.

IF there is one thing which an Englishman dislikes more than asking the way, it is having to show his passport. The unspoken suggestion that he may not have the right to be where he is, always annoys him. Women, perhaps, will always rather enjoy the *mot*. There is a certain amount of "thrill" about not being able to get past a barrier without leaning from a car and whispering "Albert " or "Mons" into a sentinel's ear; but a man likes to shout "Ongley" and drive on.

One day I remember going for a considerable journey with a delightful friend whose knowledge of French was limited, and with whom I had a varied drive. Our horn was a poor thing, evidently afflicted with a cold in its head; so instead of using it, my friend always yelled "A droite" to every car or wagon that we overtook; and not only so, but expressed a wish that I should do the same. I fear the "madness" of the English may have stamped itself anew upon our foreign cousins as we sat side by side shouting lustily.

But the real trouble was at the barriers, where we believed we ought to have been sufficiently well known to pass unchallenged. And the only thing by which my companion could explain having to produce his papers was that the guard must have recently been changed.

We both fumbled in the depths of our clothing for *laissez-passers* and identification cards, while my friend murmured wrathfully to the guard, "Vous etes nouveau; vous etes nouveau."

Another friend took me into France with no equipment in the way of language except two words, which I understood him to say were French, and to every sentry and at every barrier or gateway he remarked conversationally, "Poor Cally," and then drove on.

I began to feel sorry for some one unknown who was so evidently to be pitied. Of course, we never asked the way! and returning very late on an absolutely black night, my guide could only fix his bearings by the colours of the houses he had passed on his outward

66

journey. I used to hear him say to himself, "I know we turned off at a blue house;" and the car would swing round again, until at last directions were asked and never understood.

A knowledge of French was not the most marked characteristic of the English in Belgium, and it only became fluent when talking to a *Flamand* who was unable to understand any tongue but his own.

The number of wounded who passed through the station increased very much as the weeks went by, and it became difficult to leave the kitchen. The daily stream of suffering men began to have something very ghastly about it. The trains (which were now provided with *brancard* carriages, and priests in charge of the wounded, and stoves, etc.) were far more comfortable than they had been at first. But they were, alas, much fuller! Also, they were made to leave the station much more quickly than had been the case in earlier days— because of the shelling that went on—and there was not time to speak a word to anyone. One never saw again the men who passed before one in such an endless stream. One never knew how they fared, or whether they recovered or not. One fed them and they went on.

I cannot tell how many men used now to pass through the station, but I understood that the trains which left three times in the day held 230 men, and certainly they were often full and sometimes overcrowded.

The worst cases, of course, were those who had been left longest untended. And it was wonderful to me how some of these survived. I remember one man who had lain for four days in a trench half full of ice-cold water with both his legs broken, who did very well in the hospital afterwards. Another who had not been found for eight days was still living, but he died later. He was a particularly fine-looking young fellow, and we were all full of regret that he had not pulled through.

About this time Fumes became rather an un-healthy place! There still continued to be no regular bombardment, but the whiz of shells was not uncommon, and there were some very sad casualties. Some French friends of mine used to say, "Bon soir, pas d'obus," in much the same way as at home one says, "Sleep well!" A fine morning always brought the Taube out. One day I remarked to the woman who usually cleaned my bedroom that she had forgotten to do it. She replied, "Mais, mademoiselle, il y a un Taube qui se promene au-dessus de la maison, et j'ai peur de monter en haut."

It was a novel excuse for not cleaning a room, but a very genuine one. I liked the *qui se pro-mene* which described the flight of an aeroplane. The pigeons on the church roofs were always the first to see a Taube coming. They seemed to know by sight their hateful brothers, and fluttered with a flash of terrified white wings far away.

Even children knew the different aeroplanes by sight, and when I used to return home at night, a little French girl was always able to inform me how many bombs had fallen during the day and how many had burst. One could see that she had the smallest possible opinion of those which *ne s' lelatent pas!*

We had a sad business at the station one day when a number of men working on the line and some soldiers were looking at an aeroplane that hovered overhead and were nearly all killed by a shell. It all happened in a moment, and it produced a very painful impression upon those of us who worked in the place.

Also, it began to be evident that a station liable to bombardment was not the place for wounded men to lie. A story gained credence at the time that a spy always gave notice of the arrival and departure of trains. I do not know whether this was true or not, but I fancy there was something queer going on, and I can't envy the man or the woman who could deliberately direct an enemy's fire on helpless wounded men.

One is always sorry for the soldier to whom one sometimes hears the question put: "What does it feel like to be under fire?" My own impression is that anything descending from above is, subconsciously, so intimately associated in one's mind with a fall of rain, that it is difficult not to seek some singularly inadequate shelter where one feels perfectly safe. And I well remember going and standing under a glass roof for some time while shelling was going on! Men have told me that to get inside the canvas tilt of an ambulance makes them feel quite secure! I remarked to a friend that at Antwerp, as we crossed the road to the hospital under very heavy fire, I was glad I had an umbrella; but she never saw the little joke.

I always thought Furnes rather a weird little place, but that may have been because I so often walked through it after dark. The Grand Place is certainly lovely; but there is a good deal about Furnes that is small and rather mean-looking.

Some of our party at this time went out to Pervyse to establish a *poste au secours* there. I went out to see them once, and I wish I was able to tell more at first hand about their interesting work there. The fleeting glimpse I had of them (very uncomfortably established in the remains of a house in a ruined village, in which hardly a roof was untouched) gave me a very high opinion of their tenacity and pluck.

One approached the village by a long straight line of trees, at the end of which stood a haggard-looking church like a sentinel with both eyes shot out. Nothing was left but a blind stare. The tower had great holes in it; the aisles had fallen; and in the debris one saw twisted iron and fragments of carved masonry. The churchyard looked as though some devil had stalked through it, tearing up crosses and digging up graves. Even the dead are not left undisturbed in war! And many a body, long since committed to the dust, was disinterred by deep-burrowing shells.

Many persons believed that ladies should not expose themselves to the dangers that so constantly threatened Pervyse; but they not only did so, but remained till the place was bombarded.

As a convoy we were much less together than I anticipated. Much of the work was scattered, and the absence of a general mess, where one might have learned the doings of the various members, makes it difficult to write anything more than a personal narrative.

I saw more of the hospital staff than of any other, and I was daily struck by their efficiency, and daily impressed by their attention to duty and the good work that they did. All the nurses gave their services gratuitously; and I need hardly say that I found this out for myself, for no one ever mentioned the fact! Always, about the hospital, there was a friendliness which, I am quite sure, many strangers appreciated and will always remember. The simple hospitality that was extended to every one who arrived there, the good temper of those who had extra work to do, and the never-failing courtesy of the staff were very conspicuous at a time when so many people had no spare time to attend to anything.

The hospital had to contend with all the difficulties which attend a big undertaking of this sort at any time. And there were, besides, those perfectly "unnecessary difficulties" which, I think, nearly every one noticed during the war, and whose origin it is difficult to trace. But nothing was ever allowed to hinder the work. And it may interest those who subscribed to the hospital to know that waste of any sort was unknown. The mess was run at less than a franc per head a day, and the food was always abundant.

I always liked the way in which the hospital opened its doors before it was half ready, because wounded men wanted to come in. And so long as there was space to lay a stretcher on the floor, I don't think anyone was ever refused admittance.

When the spring came, with its floods and its cold, the long war became a long wait, where for months men stood in open graves looking at a mud wall in front of them and trying to keep their feet dry.

One night there was some severe trench fighting, and the station was very full that night. A young French officer, wounded in the head, came and sat by the kitchen fire; and I was interested to listen to his account of the fight, and to notice how much a man will say when he has only been for an hour out of the trenches, and to contrast his early account of a fight with those later accounts which are sent "to cheer up the missus," and which appear afterwards in the pages of the morning papers.

The French boy by the kitchen fire was not laughing. He was covering his face with his hands, and saying, "Oh, it was awful—awful!"

And war is awful. Recruiting will go on all the better if men know they are not going to lay down their lives for a merry picnic, and that they are not going to join the army when the war is "nearly over."

But when they know that men are covered with blood, and moaning, and that the agony of a shattered limb is not to be measured by words, then they will respond till there are no fighting men left in England; because, when comrades are falling, one must be with them. And when death comes in a horrible form, and boys with their beards hardly grown are standing up to it grim and steady, then they will want to do their bit too, if I know anything at all about it.

I went home for a fortnight's holiday, and found every one working hard and rather fond of "spy" stories. But I was much struck by the dignity of acceptance of a terrible time which I saw on all sides.

It was strange to find oneself down in the country driving about respectable, quiet lanes, and I realized, as I had not done before, that one had grown accustomed to hearing the sound of firing nearly every day.

The only thing that was difficult to accept was the often-made statement that England "did not realize" the war. If it was so, I believe that the insistent optimism of the Press had something to do with it, and the ragtime letters from the front! Of course, this had its excellent side; but war as a "good time" seems to me simply ridiculous.

The number of people in deep mourning was deeply impressive, and the still, settled look on the women's faces was as tragic and as fine as anything I have ever seen. One felt that to have spoken to them of their losses would have been worse than sending a "card of sympathy." Their best had gone for ever, from homes which would never be even a little happy again, and it seemed to me then that one didn't need to be in Belgium to realize war, but that in its deepest intensity one saw it written on the faces of wives and mothers in England.

When I got back again, I heard that Furne was being heavily shelled, and that the hospital had moved to Hoogstadt, and every one was being evacuated. I do not fancy it was too soon. One of our nurses was, alas! killed by a shell; and although all of them volunteered to remain, it was deemed advisable to shift quarters, and most people were sent, in the meantime, to La Panne and to Dunkirk. There was, however, a considerable section of the English colony who remained on at Fumes; and I heard afterwards that one might have flown the British flag from every house in the place, so touched were the Belgians by the devotion of their allies.

The number of casualties in the little town was sad indeed; and a girl of our party had a dreadful experience, being called into a humble house near the canal where two old people sitting by their fire had had their heads blown off. The ambulances were busy all the time, and houses which we knew well were completely wrecked.

The villa where I myself had stayed all the winter, and in which, through the kindness of a Belgian doctor and his wife, I had been given a room, had all its windows broken by the impact of a shell, which destroyed the house next to it. This villa is connected in all our minds with our first days at Furnes. We found it empty, and by permission it was commandeered by us. It had only three beds in it, and we were then a party of eighteen persons! Even mattresses were scarce, but we settled down as we could, and my only regret was for the usage the poor villa got. We found it just as the Belgians to whom it belonged had fled from it, and it used to remind us of some house dug out of the ruins of Pompeii in which everything had been left suddenly. The cooking pot was on the stove, and a child's toys on the table, and some wine-glasses remained as they had been left. Here we established ourselves for a time. I grieve to say that the villa was neither very tidy nor very clean after our large party had been there. There were so many overcoats and so much mud, and so many thick boots to bring it in! Picture nails may sometimes serve as clothes pegs. But I think I never before so fully appreciated the Scriptural injunction to put candles on candlesticks! The cover of a kitchen tin is *not* a good substitute, and every one knows how disreputable an empty bottle can look by daylight. Now, a Belgian lady's house is always the last word in cleanliness and order, and I shall not soon forget the horror of the poor doctor's wife when she returned. Nearly all of us were obliged to find lodgings elsewhere and madame and her sisters scrubbed and scoured the villa ceaselessly for a week. At the end of that time I heard a simple good man say that, on returning to the villa for something, he had noticed the "woman's touch" everywhere.

I feel sure that many people think that cleanliness and order can be restored by waving a wand!

There was no real settlement in Furnes after it had been bombarded. The large hospital became a sort of dressing-station, where two young doctors and our commandant remained all the time, and several of the chauffeurs remained with them. A small house on the Ypres road was found for some of the staff. The soup kitchen moved to Adenkerke station, and La Panne, which is near by, provided lodging for the rest of us.

CHAPTER IX.

LA PANNE.

LA PANNE is a pleasant little seaside place amongst the dunes; it has probably never before been inhabited in the winter. All the little villas in the place—and they are set on every sand heap—are designed for summer visitors, and there is rather a nice sea frontage, with good hotels.

The largest of these has been turned into a hospital, which is governed and controlled by Dr. de Page, the physician to the Queen of the Belgians. There are a large number of English nurses there, and as far as an unprofessional eye like my own is able to judge, it seems to be excellently managed, and to provide the utmost comfort that is possible for the wounded. The big drawing-room overlooking the sea, the balconies, and the cheerful outlook make the hospital peculiarly attractive.

On Easter Sunday the drawing-room became a chapel for the services of the English Church, and the nurses, with their usual skill in arranging and designing things out of nothing, had contrived a white altar in ascending tiers, and this was literally covered with beautiful flowers. The fragrance of them recalled England and all that it means to most of us, in a manner that was very poignant, and I suppose I may say very tender too. Flowers have been a rare sight during the war in Belgium, and the scent of pheasant-eyed narcissi and white stocks conjured up a thousand memories.

I think all the English in La Panne came to the Easter service, which, in its own simple way, struck me as being a very beautiful one.

There were men in khaki, and rows of nurses with spotless white kerchiefs covering their heads, and at the far end of the room was the high white altar laden with its flowers, and outside, seeming to encircle us, was the dim and peaceful sea.

It seemed to me that on Easter morning one was very near all those who had suffered and had lost, and all those who had died for their country in this war. It was the first Resurrection Morning, as far as we know, for many whom we had held very dear. And we thought of the boys who were gone—not indeed as angels with white wings, but as we used to know them—newly promoted to a "topper," perhaps (for, alas! so many of them were very young), or in their white cricket flannels at Eton or at Lord's. We remembered all the pleasantness of them, their fine frankness and even their excellent manners, and the clean, good lives of most of them, and their aspirations which they never were able to speak about, and their games of which they spoke so much. We thought of their fathers and mothers, and we hoped humbly and sincerely that they would know somehow that we were thinking of them, and wishing we could help them.

No doubt all of us prayed for some measure of comfort and consolation for the desolate wives too. Many of us could recall marriages of recent dates, and could see again some church crowded with friends, and a group of bridesmaids near the door; or we heard, like an echo, the band in the Guards Chapel, and saw the men lining the aisle, and the bridegroom in uniform, with some good pal beside him, waiting by the chancel steps.

That was only a year, two years ago, or not much more. But last December, perhaps, or later still, in March, we heard that "he was last seen waving his sword," or was "first into the trenches."...

They put a wooden cross up where he fell.

We thought much, too, of the men and the women who have learned to love each other better as the years go on. There is, we believe something singularly faithful and loyal about soldier's love for his wife. Most of them has "taken the rough with the smooth"— the plains of India or the dull provincial town. They face everything together, whether it is on small means or bad climates. And where English officer and his wife go there is never much amiss.

They will not be forgotten, these men of high honour and courage, whom their regiments loved and whom their men followed into hell fire We knew them in the old days, riding their ponies at regimental races or playing polo in the sun; and we knew them in South Africa, "hunting De Wet," and singing songs (for they were fifteen years

75

younger then) about the " Soldier; of the Queen." It was always "Soldiers of the Queen" in South Africa, and not "Tipperary." We knew all the cheeriness of them, and the good fellowship, and the idealism, too—for it leaked out sometimes—and we thanked them for making England what it is. They faced most things buthely, and often went into danger for the sheer fun of the thing! We think they were not afraid when they were called upon to meet the last enemy, which is Death; and if they were, they were "too well-bred to show it."

The news of the fighting at Neuve Chapelle reached us in very small supplies, and no doubt as much of it was known in England as at the front. It seemed to me to be a terrible victory. But I heard on all sides that it had "bucked" our men, who had grown tired of doing nothing. The spirit of every one seems to have been excellent, and I know that success in war cannot always be measured by territory.

We heard such news as came through about the fighting in the Dardanelles. All the newspapers I was able to obtain cried victory, and perhaps cried it too soon. For even victory may come as an anti-climax when all the big adjectives have been used up to describe the preliminaries of a great engagement.

The time at La Panne passed quietly. It is a brighter place than Fumes, and the lengthening spring days added much to the cheerfulness of every one. One saw this in the soldiers, who enjoyed games with roars of laughter in the sandy streets; and the element of personal discomfort was much lessened for every one by the milder atmosphere which now prevailed.

A Scotsman under very heavy fire said, in a tone of real North-country grumbling, "Shells make it uncomfortable for every one." There was an almost complete absence of shells in La Panne, but Taubes often arrived, and were not much regarded by anyone.

They came out of the blue on any fine morning, and generally rather early, when the soldiers were washing. The Belgians are as fond cold water as their English allies, and the soldiers can turn out looking neat after a night spent upon straw. At La Panne every villa filled with them; one can hear the sound life beginning about six o'clock, or even earlier when the sky is pale green before the dawn and the men kindle fires—orange red against the quiet early morning light. While they are busy *on annonce* a Taube by the blowing of a steam syren; a few heavy-footed, elderly women begin to run, and children are told to come indoors as one tells them to come in out of a shower. The pigeons, of course, are annoyed. They hate and fear the giant over head, and fly from every steeple. Some whit tufts appear in the sky, followed, perceptibly later, by the sound of bursting shells. The soldiers, washing themselves in little villa gardens, stop their ablutions for a moment, and with hands above their eyes or caps held at arm's length to keep off the glare, look up into the sky for a moment, and then go on with their washing. The syren continues to whistle, and some people get out of bed to look at the Taube, and some lie still.

I think that, to the British mind, there has always been something a little comic about German aircraft.

One day at Adenkerke station we saw one turned back by the fire that met it, and later, one of our friends saw a strange sight. The returning Taube was greeted by a rain of shells, and in the midst of this and in the thick of it a British and a French aeroplane came out and hovered over it like birds of prey, and fired upon it, and it burst into flames and fell to earth like a stone.

Both men were dead and charred beyond all recognition....

About this time the work of the kitchen spread a little, because of the number of *malades* and *eclopes* who came to Adenkerke for a brief rest. A sick soldier is as deserving of sympathy as a wounded one. And yet, naturally perhaps, he does not get half the attention in war time that the other does. It seems to me that a man in good health can bear a great deal of pain and discomfort, but the man who has " gone sick " does not know what to make of himself or what is wrong. As a rule, he is suffering either from too much work or too little food, and he often has to put up with a long spell of suffering before the ambulances, which are instantaneous in their services on the wounded, come to take him away.

At the Pavilion St. Vincent at Adenkerke all the *&lopes* used to come and rest. They were men for the most part with "little ailments"—sore feet, toothache, earache, or such like—and a few days' rest used to do them a world of good. The warmth of the stoves alone and the long sleep they got did much to restore them. Owing to the kindness of friends one was able to supply them with all the woollen goods—socks, scarves, etc.—that they required, and I found that slippers were more appreciated than anything else. An Eastbourne work-party, a Craigmillar work-party, and a mothers' meeting work-party at Chart Sutton kept me well supplied.

It is impossible to leave La Panne without saying something about a little hospital which established itself just opposite the station where I worked. It belonged to Lady Bagot, and I always thought that there was something particularly attractive about it—a quietness and serenity that was good for sick people. The one plain wooden ward, with its well-scrubbed boards, had a friendly air of goodness about it, which, of course, was due to herself and her staff; and although the little brown wooden building was only a " flying " one, it always looked restful and at peace.

The soup kitchen became rather more military at Adenkerke than it had been before, and I became officially attached to the Belgian Army. Two men came on as helpers in the kitchen. It was not quite so interesting to distribute soup which one had not entirely made oneself, but the new plan did not work at all badly. The only thing that struck me (if I may venture on so horribly egoistical a remark) was that, whereas the number of wounded coming through the station was reduced, owing to the lull in the war, from hundreds a day to perhaps a hundred, the work began to be thought rather strenuous. At Fumes we did not have any regular assistance, and the Belgian Sisters and I used to think our soup and coffee rather good.

I can only imagine that it was the awful and alarming energy of the small woman that helped us. I am five feet nothing, and I was a little bit the tallest!

Meanwhile, the hospital was at Hoogstadt, and one missed one's friends of the staff, and hardly ever saw them.

I shall always retain a vision of them all in the bustling yard of the college filled with motor ambulances, all of which, whether they were running or not, tried to make as much noise as possible, and from underneath which men with rags in their hands and an odour of petrol about them used to creep unexpectedly. Every one was in a hurry and stood about with cigarettes in their mouths. There was a feeling that one had to " hop in," followed by hours of alert waiting for nothing in particular. I fancy (although I fear to say anything so daringly indiscreet) that some of those hours were taken up and fully employed by determined accusations to each other of having " bagged my things," and persistent and indignant denials of the same.

A habit of "pinching" prevails in war time which seems to affect even the most honest persons, and it is allowable to wonder whether in this respect characters may not be permanently destroyed. No property—from motor tyres to bandages—was safe!

The result of this was that every one used to go about with all their portable goods in their pockets. This gave them a very bulgy appearance. Doubtless, however, one used to think that things carried with so much care and so carefully guarded must be of considerable value.

A turned-out pocket generally disclosed a watch that had long since stopped and never meant to go again; a fountain-pen which was not filled up, and when filled leaked; an electric torch that required a refill; a scarf which had been pinched from some one else and wanted careful watching; a store of cigarettes and no matches.

There was a convenient habit—where so many were strangers amongst us—of calling men by the names of the cars which they drove, and one of them was always known even to the servants as "Monsieur le Pipe"—a name which exactly suited him.

A foreign chauffeur called the "Goat" always seemed to have a strange and deleterious effect upon all persons with whom he came in contact. No one ever went for a drive with the "Goat" without coming back a worse man. Tempers, otherwise serene, were so effectually disturbed by him that they did not recover for hours afterwards, and language failed when speaking of or to the "Goat."

On the only journey I ever made with him he seemed to be suggesting at every barrier that I was a German spy, and I think he was the most timid creature I have ever met. Why we were not all arrested and shot, on the evidence of his manner alone, I do not know.

He had a car which always seemed to be part of him, and without which it is impossible to picture him. It was lined in an unusual manner with window muslin with blue flowers on it. It went loudly and slowly all its days, and was famous for being passed by every one on the road.

Personally I don't believe that anyone but the "Goat" could have knocked a single spark out of it! He used to spend all his days with his head inside the bonnet, coaxing and flattering the engine which he loved, and at night he slept, with all the windows up, inside the car.

I have a lurking suspicion that he hated us as much as we hated him. He wanted to speak to his engine all day, and we wanted him to drive; and when we thoroughly understood each other in this matter, it did not make for peace.

There was a good fellow who was very much liked by us, whom we used to call "Boots," because of the very thick ones he wore. They used to take complete charge of the wearer and marched him about where they listed. Their weight was so great that in coming downstairs they seemed to act like weights pulling him from step to step, and they had a determined and unyielding look about them, which gave one the impression that they led the wearer and not he them.

"Boots" had a passion for makeshifts, and was never so happy as when he was contriving something out of nothing or diverting things from their original purpose. He was not really contented except when he was splitting up old boxes to serve some wise and great end; and he slept in a storeroom behind a blackboard, and had his bath in a waterproof sheet stretched over a motor tyre.

Many people indulged, as English people abroad always seem to do, in unusual clothing, and a shower of rain, for instance, would produce oilskins and sou'westers, which no fishermen on the wettest day in the west of Scotland could have beaten.

Belgium is wet, but the size of our boots was designed for a flood, and we affected hats of uncompromising sternness.

Some of the ladies wore knitted caps in which they looked very nice, I thought. But no mountain-climber, no lady pig-sticker or huntress of wild beasts ever wore clothing so abnormally practical as we did. It even soared, in some cases, to masculinity. And a certain guileless maiden lady always nervously explained to Belgian officers that English ladies did not as a general rule dress in breeches and gaiters.

The kindly Belgians explained it all in their polite way by saying that "Les Anglaises sont pratiques."

It has been said that England is bound in the best portmanteau leather. Straps, certainly, assist one much, and I am quite sure may even help some people to feel heroic. But the khaki and the straps and the gaiters came to be associated in people's minds with very good practical work, and very plucky work too. "The only real danger," as I heard a young girl in puttees say, "will be when we return to London and fall over tight skirts."

CHAPTER X.

LA PANNE.

THE weather continued cold but bright at La Panne. The lengthening days were a great delight, and spring came late, but with a wealth and a marvel of green. A wind was blowing in from the sea, and lilacs nodded from over the hedges. The tender corn rustled its delicate little chimes, and all across it the light breezes sent arpeggio chords of delicate music, like a harp played on silver strings. A big horse-chestnut tree burst suddenly into bloom and carried its flowers proudly like a bouquet, and the shy hedges put up a screen all laced and decorated with white may. It seemed as though Mother Earth had become young again, and was tossing her babies up to the summer sky, while the wind played hide-and-seek or peep-bo or some other ridiculous game with them. Only the guns boomed all the time, and the Belgians, quiet and patient as always, and the little French *marins,* with their charming manners, and the Zouaves, wholly contemptuous of wounds and of suffering, came in as before into the little station, and sat in the big hall there and talked very little, and in the evening the train was filled up as usual with them. The ambulances, with their brown canvas tilts, came in as they had always done, and fresh graves were dug in the spring sunshine.

Mother Earth, with her new-born babies, used to stop playing then for a time and tell us that it was all right; and when a little procession used to come along the road with its humble burden carried shoulder high, she who is never unsympathetic as some would have us believe used to whisper, "They have come back to me, as all my children do: the leaves next autumn, and the boys perhaps to-morrow."...

The work was not nearly so heavy as it had been, and one began to have some leisure. Two friends of mine, who play beautifully, used to come to practise duets on the piano at the villa where I lodged, and a great deal of pleasure it gave me. A painter, invalided for a time from the trenches, made some excellent portraits; and Monsieur de la Haye, the well-known war artist and a member, of the Paris Salon, was constantly at work with his sketch-book at the station, making some of his vigorous and splendid drawings.

I suppose I ought to have known it, but as a matter of fact I had never realized before that art flourishes in Belgium like a plant in a fair soil. It seems as natural for a Belgian to be a painter or a musician as it is for him to sleep or to eat. Even the soldiers whistle in tune, and in a manner more melodious than I have ever heard, and everywhere one finds a love of pictures and an intimate knowledge of music. Sometimes I fancied that the want of art in some other nations produces a feeling of genuine wonder in the minds of our allies. To know a good picture, for instance, is with them an instinct, and nothing more terribly enforces the realization of the loss which they have sustained in the destruction of their beautiful buildings than to discover (as one was doing every day in Belgium) that these had been not merely national memorials, to be shown off with pride to strangers, but the household gods of a people to whom beauty is a natural expression far more than a studied part.

Everywhere one was getting evidence of it! A soldier begs for a stump of pencil, and fills one's sketch-book with some inimitable studies of faces; and a musician, who ought to be laid up as a treasure in heaven, delights one with his music on one evening and goes back into the trenches the next!

After a short period of leisure came a busy time again. There had been a great deal of heavy fighting, and some villages subjected to bombardment had paid the usual toll in the matter of wounded and killed civilians. Every one has noticed the seeming indifference with which the inhabitants of Flanders—or all that remains of it—appear to regard the dangers of war. It has been the greatest difficulty with those who have had charge of refugee work to persuade villagers and dwellers in little hamlets to leave their farms and cottages; and I have often heard it said, by men who have seen and had wide experience of the struggle that is now going on, that nothing has ever made them so astonished as seeing some old Belgian woman, in her black knitted cap, calmly hoeing turnips or digging up potatoes quite close to the firing-line, or while shelling has been going on.

Always, these simple villagers are the last to leave a stricken neighbourhood, and even when every one else has fled, it is quite a common sight to see them sitting at their doors, having appeared from heaven knows where, and enjoying the evening sunshine, with their children about them, long after every one else has moved away to safer quarters.

There is one woman with four little children who has lived in a tiny house near the canal at Nieuport ever since that much-bombarded place was subjected to shell fire. It is hardly too much to say that a more dangerous position would be hard to find. The fields all round are pitted with shell holes, and woods and trees, and even the roadway, have suffered throughout a wide area for many months past. The Flemish woman stays on in her little cottage, and I am told that children in Flanders often take food to the trenches.

I remember particularly one evening at Adenkerke when many wounded civilians were being brought in from Ypres, Poperinghe, and various places in the neighbourhood. There was an ambulance filled with wounded children, for whom, I think, King Herod himself might have been sorry if he had seen them. They were such tiny things to be already in the war! And they were lifted out of the ambulance wagons with their arms and legs in splints, or with their little curly heads bandaged. Two little mites, sitting on a long, full-sized stretcher, gazed solemnly at each other, and each was evidently filled with wonder at the unusual appearance of his little neighbour. There were sad tales to tell about nearly all of them. This baby had been found in a house, and no one could tell where his mother was. And that one had escaped death in some marvellous way when her parents and her grandmother were killed. One little creature of three weeks old lay in the hospital for a long time with both its feet wounded. He was "Albert," as all the children in Belgium are now, and Albert's young mother had died on the operating table, being, as they told me, riddled with wounds.

One asked oneself whether this was not frightfulness enough, while sorrowfully aware that one had seen only a very small portion of the suffering and the wrongs which have befallen Belgium.

The scene at the railway station seemed to focus itself into an extraordinary picture. The railway lines run due west, and at the far end of them, where the gleaming rails seem to converge, the sun was setting in a sky of extraordinary splendour. There were level rays of light which made the station in the unattractive little town look almost picturesque for the moment, and all along the platform were lying stretchers with women and children on them. The women were brown-haired, decent-looking young matrons, and it grieved one very deeply to see these innocent victims of what can only be called devilry. The long Red Cross compartment of the train was first of all filled with the children, and the usual Englishman in khaki appeared carrying something with him. He shoved it down in a corner with the usual guilty look of an Englishman doing a little bit of kindness, and we found a box of groceries and sweet biscuits and milk, and everything that a little party of invalids could want on their long journey to Switzerland. Some young Belgian soldiers meanwhile had got into the train, and were making friends with the babies, and afterwards the women were brought in also. Presently the train moved slowly off, and one could hear the plaintive crying of children who were going to bed in these strange quarters without, alas! their mothers to tuck them up; and one caught a glimpse once more, as one said goodbye, of the outstretched forms of the women. It occurred to one, as it has occurred to many people both at home and abroad, that it does not do to look at war too closely. Far away one may sing songs about it, but there were too many suffering people in Belgium!

It was touching to see a little family of terrified children and their mother sheltering in a roadside Calvary one day when the shells were coming over. The young mother was holding up her baby for protection to the Figure on the Cross, and some little toddling creatures were clinging about her skirts.

A Belgian officer told us that the most awful thing he had ever had to do was to order his men to fire on a German regiment which was protecting itself behind his own countrywomen.

Some of our corps were evacuating the women and children at a small village, and one man, seeing his wife and daughter stretched out on the ground, went mad, and ran up and down the field screaming. One saw a good deal of mad-ness on all sides.

Another of our corps was helping to carry in on a stretcher a young girl whose shoulder had been shot away, and who was dying. A young Belgian peasant, who walked in front of my friend, helping to carry the stretcher, turned round and said quietly, "This is my fiancée."

A dying French soldier, once measuring six feet four inches, and now lying with both his legs amputated, looked up and said, smiling to a friend of mine, "I used often to complain, mademoiselle, that my bed was too short, but I shan't have to grumble about that now." His old father and mother arrived to see him just after he had breathed his last.

One almost envied the people of whom one heard it said that they had not begun to realize yet!

Once there came a sort of British morning, with a fresh British breeze blowing over the feathered tops of the waves; and as I stood on the sands at La Panne, I saw one of our own men-of-war blazing away at the coast. The Germans answered by shells which fell rather wide, and must have startled the fishes (but no one else) by the splash they made. There were long, swift torpedo-boats, with two great white wings of cloven foam at their bows, and a flourish of it in their wake, moving along under a canopy of their own black smoke. It being a British day, one was fatuous enough to glory in the fact that even the coal was British, and to tell oneself that one knew where it came from, and to picture once more the grimy workmen who dwell in the Black Country and get it out of the ground. The man-of-war in front of us was burning plenty of it, and when she had done her work she put up a banner of smoke and steamed away with a splendid air of dignity across the white-flecked sea. One knew the men on board of her! Probably not a heart beat faster by a second for all the German shells; probably dinner was served as usual, and men had their tubs and got their clothes brushed when it was all over.

I went down to my kitchen a little late, but I had seen something that Drake never saw—a bit of modern sea-fighting!

In the evening when I returned the long gray man-of-war was there again. The sun was westering now, and the sea had turned to gold, and the gray hull looked black against the glare. But the fire of the man-of-war's guns was brighter than the evening sunset; and she was a spitfire after all, this dignified lady, for she " let 'em have it! " while the long, lean torpedo boats looked on.

About this time (because I was coming home to lecture at various ammunition centres) I was given permits to see one or two places which interested me very much. And most of all, I think, I was impressed by visiting Nieuport, which I had not seen since last November. It was like coming back and finding a friend much worse than one had anticipated. Some one said to me, " Ypres smells of lilac and of death." I do not think there were any lilacs at Nieuport. The place was too shockingly destroyed for that. Everywhere about it there was the most extraordinary atmosphere of desolation and destruction. So many shells had fallen on the bare earth and on the fields all round it, on which no harvest was ripening, that I can only describe them by saying that they looked like immense Gruyere cheeses pitted with holes.

But indeed it is as difficult to find words to describe Nieuport as it is to talk of metaphysics in slang. The words do not seem to be invented that will convey the sense of desolation of the spot, or the supreme and aching quiet of it under the shock of constantly firing guns. Hardly anything is left now of the little homely things that, when I saw the place last time, reminded one that this was once a city of living human beings. Then, one saw a few interiors, exposed, it is true, and damaged, but still of this world; now, it is one big grave—the grave of a city and the grave of many of its inhabitants.

At a corner house nine ladies lie under the piled-up debris that once made their home. In another, some soldiers met their death, and some crumbling bricks were heaped over them too. The houses have all fallen; some outer walls remain, but I hardly saw a roof left, and everywhere there are empty window frames and skeleton rafters. I never knew so surely before that a town can live and can die. At Nieuport there is not a heart-beat left to throb in it. Thousands of shells have fallen into it, and continue to fall.

And at night the nightingale sings there, and by day the river flows gently under the ruined bridge. Every tree in the wood near by is torn and beheaded; hardly one has a top remaining. The new green pushes out amongst the blackened trunks. One found oneself speaking low in Nieuport—the place was so horribly dead.

The streets, heaped up with debris and full of shell holes, were bright with sunlight, but were quite deserted. From the cellars in some ruined buildings, whose insecure walls looked as though they might totter and fall any minute, some Zouaves or an occasional French *marin* appeared.

Most of these ran out with letters in their hands for us to post. God knows what they can have had to write about from that grave!

In the cathedral and amongst its crumbling, battered walls a strange peace rests, and one notices—what scores of people have already noticed in Belgium—that in the midst of the ruins there nearly always stands one sacred figure, which, when everything else has fallen, holds out pitiful arms in some shrine. In a little house almost entirely fallen, and with its remaining walls blackened by fire, I found a tragic-looking little crucifix still upon the walls. This I asked to keep. It must once have been very well carved, I think, and there was an extraordinary expression on the clear-cut face, while the broken limbs reminded me of much that I had seen during the war. Over the cathedral doorway the figures of a crowned Mother and her Child remain almost untouched, while almost at her feet there was a little graveyard filled with crosses where the dead lie. A shell had entered, and torn some bones from their resting-place, and these lay amongst a few simple flowers which some soldier had laid on the graves.

We went to see the dim cellars with their vaulted roofs which form the two *pontes au secours*. In the inner recess a doctor has a bed, and there was a table with a vase of scarlet peonies upon it. In the outer cave some soldiers were eating. There is no light there, even during the day, except from the doorway. The sunlight outside looked blinding compared with the deep shadows within.

Mrs. Wynne comes every night and most afternoons to this *poste,* driving her own ambulance without lights of any sort, and removing the wounded who wait for her there to the French hospital at Zuitecote. All through the winter, and whether the road has been shelled or not, she has always been there with a chauffeur and one of the gentlemen of our ambulance corps, who has a curious preference for shell fire. I hope that she will not think it an impertinence on my part to praise her work, or to record that it was always done with simplicity and courage.

We wandered about Nieuport for a considerable time in the unearthly quiet which persisted, even when guns began to blaze away close by us, sending their whizzing shells over our heads; and we walked down to the river, and saw the few boards which are all that remain of the bridge. As we came away from the place in the gloaming, a bird broke into a rapture of song quite close to us. The birds never have any fear of bursting shells, and I have often heard soldiers say that they seem to sing all the louder for the noise that is going on. From many a field of battle the larks mount up joyously, and I have heard of men making pets of robins in the trenches. There is a nightingale in a little wood in the long, uninteresting road which lies between Adenkerke and La Panne. Here every sort of vehicle is passing all day long, soldiers are marching, and there is the perpetual sound of motor horns, bugles, and the like, and in the midst of it, and especially after rain, the little brown bird in the bushes sings on undisturbed. While men are killing each other he loses himself in a burst of song that recalls all the old joyous things which one used to know. The poetry of life seems to be over for a time. The war songs are forced and sometimes a little foolish; pictures are put away in cellars, and stained glass, where it can be saved, is removed from church windows, and books are closed. But the nightingale sings on, and the old spirit of youth and of joyfulness looks out through smoke and carnage, and speaks of evenings in dim woods at home, or of dawn when one used to hear birds in the garden and turned round comfortably in some sweet-scented chintz-

89

furnished room and went to sleep again. The nightingale sings above the sound of death and of tears, and the little wood close to the tramway line becomes filled with one of those unexpected voices which one sometimes hears when one is alone.

CHAPTER XI.

FROM A KITCHEN WINDOW.

THE last chapter of a woman's book is always inclined to be a little discursive, I am afraid. She can write with that "restraint," which reviewers love to praise, throughout a volume; but in the last chapter she is apt to fall from grace a little.

From a kitchen window the great panorama of war limits itself to a view through little panes of glass—a glimpse of a limited area seen through a cloud of steam from boiling pots, and dimmed, although not necessarily distorted, by it. Bending over a stove—blackleaded and inclined to smoke—one may think of many things; and when one goes to the window and looks out, one may think of many more.

There was always a train in front of the window, and in the train were wounded men, and in the hospitals were wounded men, and in the ambulances, and in the waiting-rooms at the station, were more wounded men. One got more accustomed to seeing soldiers with bandages than without them, at the railway station during the war. And all were suffering, some less, some more, and nearly all were helpless. Two words began to say themselves in my head whenever the convoys of wounded came in, "Rendered inefficient." No doubt it is the main object of war, when it does not kill, to maim. But men meant to be useful, and to work and to be happy, were now limping, blind, sometimes mad, and struck off the roll of the useful ones! The sight of these impressed me very painfully, especially, I think, at night. In the dim light the thin faces had a more haggard look, and the helplessness of the men on the stretchers seemed more marked than during the day. The train used to fill up and move out of the dim station into the greater dimness beyond, and the men sat or lay in the unlighted carriages, each one silent and holding an injured limb.

The death-roll was very long, and one saw, day after day, labelled humanity with a number on it passing in an endless succession upon blood-stained stretchers. It was not the exception but the rule to see them. Naturally, it influenced one's vision. Naturally, the writing of others who saw the life of soldiers in camp will bear a very different complexion. My own experience was much like that of persons who stand on the beach while others put out to sea, and at whose feet pieces of wreck and corpses are thrown up by the tide. The excitement of the heart of the storm is not for them, they only see the results of it. And the results are so pitiful in their dumbness and their loneliness, and in their pain! One scruples to wring the hearts of those who are already doing all they can do, by a mere recital of things sad, and one fears still more to say anything that might even remotely savour of being sensational; but there is no one with the smallest amount of imagination who cannot picture to himself what men who have been exposed to shell-fire or a rain of shrapnel, and who have come out of it alive, are like.

The woman's view is almost bound to obtrude itself from a kitchen window. And women are asking many questions now. In the sorrow which has come to many of them they, who are not prone to complain, may even be asking themselves whether territory and commerce and treasure, and all those other things which men call " property," should perpetually demand the sacrifice of what in a very peculiar way belongs to them. The loss of the lives of their sons will always appear to women to be too high a price to pay for anything the world contains or is able to produce. The whole idea of the value of life is inherent in them. A woman probably never thinks of a boy as an eldest son or as an inheritor of lands, but merely as a great joy which came first. It is hard to part with him. And there comes a moment when she stands protesting passionately that she has had no voice in the making of war, and she rebels utterly and absolutely against having to pay this unthinkable price for it. In the almost unbearable pain of loss she demands to know, what is the logical connection between boys with their lungs shot through and their heads blown off, and a madman's greed for territory and power? Sitting by some sick-bed when the candles are burning low, she seeks some explanation of the sheer, horrible idiocy of the whole thing.

She asks, what does a boy of eighteen really know about commerce or world-power? But they put him into a trench half-full of cold water, and plugged down iron and steel upon him, and sent him down to the station with a number on his breast, or back to the old house in the country where he was born, and where he lies on his back all through the spring days. What, again, does a little Belgian soldier know of the gambler playing for high stakes, who tried to take up a little country as he would gather up a small coin off the gaming-table? The little Belgian soldier lies buried where he fell, and his womenkind also may be asking themselves whether there ever was a more mad way of settling a quarrel than to put a lump of lead into their boy's lungs.

They demand, as of old, "Where shall wisdom be found?" And the reply is still the same: "Destruction and death say, It is not in me."

They do not blame anyone for this war except the man who brought it about. Even they know that it must be fought, and fought to the end. But on broader lines they ask whether war itself must not come to an end, and whether men of reason and nations of reason may not settle their quarrels and their differences like sober and reasonable beings. They deny that a need to kill is a male instinct, and they know men who tell them that when a fine morning comes they hate to go out and do each other to death.

They have heard—who has not heard—that this war is a war of metals and of oil, of petrol bubbling in engines and steel hurtling through the air, and the almost naïve question which they put is this: "Why not then eliminate the human element altogether?" Let the gun that can throw farthest fire its shells against so much thickness of masonry or so much strength of iron plates. Why bring young men and boys into the matter? A little German in spectacles, ten miles away, may be an excellent marks-man, and when war really becomes a matter of artillery and ammunition, let him blaze away in the most approved method at some distant mark or target.

Women's questions are proverbially difficult to answer. And the odd part of it is, that they so often get a hearing. One trembles to write so big a thing, but the abolition of war may be one of the tasks which will in the future belong to them, and will be settled by them. Meanwhile the Dominion of Force puzzles them a good deal, because they so often hear its dominion contradicted or denied.

The only attitude towards this war, and towards all war, which seems inadmissible, is the one which regards it with pious horror. Firstly, because, quite calmly considered, honour is a thing of more intrinsic value than life; and secondly, because the reality of war does not lie solely in the suffering which it brings.

The reality lies in the dim old battered bugles blown up to the sky in the early morning; and the hungry men " sticking it," with their eyes grown haggard and the line of their cheek-bones standing out starkly from their faces. The reality lies with the tired men marching stolidly on, and with the sick men staying in the trenches, and with the simple soldier lying down and dying on a muddy field, and with the women laughing at shells and going to their doorways to see them.

And the reality lies also in the extraordinary sense of freedom which war brings. Because in war we are up against the biggest thing in life, and that is death. Most people fear it, but in war time a curious thing happens, and men are released from fear. This cannot be explained by merely saying they have become accustomed to danger, but in its essence it is something far greater and more profound than this. War becomes not so much a fight for freedom as in itself a freedom. And death is not a release from suffering, but a release from fear. Soldiers know this, although they can never explain it. They have been terrified. They have been more terrified than their own mothers will ever know, and their very spines have melted under the shrieking sounds of shells. And then comes the day when they "don't mind." Death stalks just as near as ever, but his face, quite suddenly, has a friendly air. Bullets and pieces of shell may come, but it doesn't matter. This is the day on which the soldier learns to stroll when the shrapnel is falling, and to look up and laugh when the bullets sing close by.

In war time all lesser disputes have an end, and it almost seems as though already we saw things from some larger standpoint and from some greater height.

From a height alone, we know that the wider view is obtainable. Thus, already we are wondering whether the trade disputes, for instance, of last year were so serious as we then thought them.

94

Already we may be saying, quite reasonably and meaning every word of it, that man cannot live by bread alone, whether it be a big loaf or a little one; and already we may be wondering at the great and momentous change which has come over not our own country only, but many other countries.

By humiliation Germany, who has already learned something, may have to learn a lesson of far more real "frightfulness" than she has been able to teach.

France has learned a noble seriousness which did not formerly belong to her, and France, believe me, is praying now, as, perhaps, she had a little bit forgotten how to pray. But she has not forgiven yet, and perhaps never will forgive. So when her turn comes, there will be trouble for those who so grievously and wantonly hurt and destroyed her!

Belgium was a little country with a potential soul. A little, exclusive, highly sensitive country, prosperous and happy, with a people who wanted to be left alone. By nature and by preference they were neutrals, until they found, what every honest-hearted nation must find, that neutrality is impossible as long as right is right and wrong is wrong. Belgium had begun, like some small clan or proud little family, to be independent, and, to use the common phrase, to "keep herself to herself." She made her own laws and had her own social life, and her own institutions, and her own way of thinking about things and of doing them. It was narrow, but it had the elements of great things in it. And then there came, as it comes to pass to all exclusive and proud people, the call to mix with men—to mix with nations. Belgium had to rub shoulders with humanity and to suffer; above all things to suffer. A tremendous re-birth had come, and a great soul was born, with a king for its father, whom the nations acknowledge as a worthy sire.

Belgium had a little distrusted the world round about her, and was not even much interested in it. And she found quite suddenly and unexpectedly that the world wanted her—that exclusiveness was no longer possible. She had done the big thing and the right thing, and she found hearts beating for her and men waiting to die with her. And the people who she thought were strangers came at a moment when trouble was at the door, and they had the faces of old friends. In her sorrow and in her ruin she has clasped hands with the world!

And what of England? She is too dear to us to criticize. Almost one fears to write of her lest the deadly things which schoolboys call " slobber " and " gush " should find their way in, and like the sickly scent of a valentine almost destroy the motto and the verse!

England had not been at her best for some time, and there is no disguising the fact. National sentiment was getting a little bit cold; military ardour certainly was not altogether the fashion; emotion was exhausting itself without any adequate results; and a queer sort of selfishness appeared to be becoming almost a national characteristic. It never went very deep, but it deceived our neighbours into thinking we were utterly degenerate. As a matter of fact, we were only going through a transition period, such as every growing child and every growing nation knows, and we had far too much energy and not quite enough to do; and when this state of affairs returns again, we may probably go through another transition period. But it will never be quite the same again, because to our national memory is added the story of Ypres, because we have spent the winter in the trenches, and because we have learned many things which are far too serious to discuss here. At the back of it all there is still in England something big to draw upon—we may call it what we like. And it is something which is not going to fail yet awhile; and which is certainly not going to fail until this war is over, and small nations are protected, and mothers get their sons again.

Meanwhile we go on learning many things. And we smile at many things too. We smile a good deal, for instance, at people who sit in chairs, holding a balance in their hands, and deciding that justice consists in keeping that balance equal; whereas, of course, justice generally demands that one side shall weigh to the ground and the other shall kick the beam. We smile a little at those who have adopted the wise and sensible course, which is seldom either wise or sensible, and have stayed at home, or have kept out of a quarrel, or are very busy pronouncing judgment upon it. We think (for we are all schoolboys in war time) that we would rather be fighting than looking on, however hard the knocks may be that we get. We do know a few things now. We know that heroes are fighting men, and not mere tillers of the soil nor mere money-getters, and we greet the parchment-faced old scribes, holding pens in their knuckled hands, and laugh with them, because of the asses' heads which they drew on the figures of the merely rich. Money and power and self-interest have been taking quite low seats lately! And we have been finding out something about national honour and other beautiful things, and discovering what freedom means, and exactly how much sacrifice courage demands, and what is worth while, and what is not.

During the war—it was almost bound to be so—there have been stories told of psychic experiences, and even of clouds that have stood between armies, and of glimpses of heavenly hosts. These may be true or they may not be true. They may be the result of men's fancy or of their imagination. But there is one vision which no one can deny, and which each man who cares to look may see for himself. It is the vision of something which lies beyond sacrifice. And in that bright and heavenly atmosphere we shall see—we may indeed see to-day—the forms of many who have fallen. We believe they fight still, although unharmed now and for evermore, but warriors still on the side of right, captains of a host which no man can number, and champions of all that we hold good. We think that when the last roll is called we shall find them still cheery, still unwavering, answering to their good names which they carried unstained through a score of fights, and still—who knows!—on active service.

THE END

BIG BYTE BOOKS is your source for great lost history!

Made in the USA
Lexington, KY
05 May 2018